POPE-POURRI

John Dollison

A Fireside Book

Published by Simon & Schuster

New York   London   Toronto   Sydney   Tokyo   Singapore

F

FIRESIDE
Rockefeller Center
1230 Avenue of the Americas
New York, NY 10020

FIRESIDE and colophon are registered trademarks
of Simon & Schuster Inc.

Designed by John Javna and John Dollison

Manufactured in the United States of America

10   9   8   7   6   5   4   3   2   1

Library of Congress Cataloging-in-Publication Data
CIP information is available.

ISBN 0-671-88615-0

To John Javna, who taught me how to write,
and to my family, who taught me how to live

ACKNOWLEDGMENTS

I would like to thank everyone whose advice and assistance made this book possible, including:

Jack Mingo

Lenna Lebovich

Sharilyn Hovind

Ed Walters

Kara Leverte

Rob Henderson

Marilyn Abraham

Suzanne Donahue

Sue Fleming

Melissa Schwarz

Derek Goldberg

Ed, Peggy, and Paul Vomund

John Harada

Kevin and Sandy McEntee

Sherry Powell

Ingo Hofmann

Anna Marie Cumisky

Jeff Perry

John Cummings, M.P.

Lee Wolfe

Steve Yung

John Holsonbake

Brian Hom

Dan Wu

Gabe Wolfenstein

Jimmy Joe 'n' Tan

Mike McDermott

Brian Pozzo

Scott and Jae Jung

Alex Markowitz

Henry Lin 'n' Fan

Frank Broccolo

German Galeota

Alex Richard

Dirk Frieser

David Yoo

Mike Brown

Tim Horn

Erik McCain

Everyone *else* at the Sammy House, Berkeley, California

De La Salle High School, Concord, California

CONTENTS

This book has two things in common with the Bible: (1) it deals with Christianity, and (2) you don't have to read the sections in order if you don't want to—you can skip straight to the parts you want to read first, and come back to the rest later. That's why the table of contents is organized according to subject.

INTRODUCTION

H ave you ever heard of the Cadaver Synod? (It was a bizarre tenth-century trial in which one pope, Stephen VI, dug up the decomposing corpse of his predecessor, Pope Formosus I, dressed it in papal robes, and put it on trial for perjury and "aspiring to the papacy.") Most Catholics haven't.

Did you know that champagne was invented *by accident* by a seventeenth-century Benedictine monk named Dom Perignon? Most Catholics don't.

Why does the pope wear a pointy hat? Most Catholics can't answer the question. And why is Saint Lucy portrayed in art carrying her eyeballs on a platter? Hardly anyone remembers anymore.

Let's face it: While this stuff is interesting, it's too trivial for the church to devote much attention to (it is *trivia*, after all)—and even if your priest wanted to teach you some Catholic Church trivia, when would he find the time? At best, most of us, even the most devout Catholics, see our priest once a week during Mass, when he has plenty of other things on his mind.

That's why I wrote this book: I wanted to talk about some of the interesting and unusual facts about the church that it doesn't have time to tell you itself. Did you know, for example, that there have been thirteen popes named Innocent? (Not all of them lived up to the title.) Or that seventeen popes have been assassinated? (Most were murdered by *other* popes.)

Controversial Subjects

This book is not a history book by any stretch of the imagination, but it does deal with topics in Catholic Church history that many well-meaning Catholics believe are best left forgotten. "Sure," they argue, "many popes, saints, and other Christians have said and done things that in the twentieth century would be considered immoral . . . and even un-Christian. Even so, it is disrespectful, not to mention bad for the church, to write about these topics."

I couldn't disagree more.

I take the same approach to Catholic Church history as I take to American history: Just as knowing about slavery makes us better Americans, so does knowing about Catholic controversies make us better Catholics. Talking about the mistakes of our past (and our present)—even in jest, as this book does—makes our faith stronger by bringing us closer to God.

Enough said. I had a *great* time working on this book. If you have half as much fun reading it as I did writing it, your money will have been well spent.

John Dollison
Berkeley, California
June 28, 1994

PAPAL BULL

*In official church parlance, a bull is an important decree issued
by the Holy Father. Some popes, however, have been known
for an entirely different kind of bull. Some examples:*

"The popes, like Jesus, are conceived by their mothers through
the overshadowing of the Holy Ghost. All popes are a certain
species of man-god. . . . All powers in heaven, as well as on earth,
are given to them."

—Pope Stephen V (885-891)

"The doctrine of the double motion of the earth about its axis and
about the sun is false, and contrary to holy scripture."

—Pope Paul V (1605-1621)

"Benito Mussolini is . . . a gift of Providence, a man free from the
prejudices of the politicians of the liberal school."

—Pope Pius XI (1922-1939)

"From the polluted fountain of indifferentism flows that absurd
and erroneous doctrine, or rather, *raving*, which claims and
defends liberty of conscience for everyone. From this comes, in a
word, the worst plague of all, namely, unrestrained liberty of opinion and freedom of speech. . . . It is in no way lawful to demand,
to defend, or to grant unconditional freedom of thought, or
speech, of writing, or of religion, as if they were so many rights
that nature has given to man."

—Pope Gregory XVI (1831-1846)

"I would have made a good Pope."

—Richard M. Nixon (1913-1994)

The first Catholic Mass in an airship took place on the *Hindenburg* on May 7, 1936.

STRANGE SCENES

Not all saints are as lucky as Francis of Assisi when it comes to art.
He's usually painted surrounded by animals or preaching to birds—
but some other saints are remembered in ways that are
downright weird. Some examples:

SAINT ROCCO (1350-1390)

How He's Portrayed: With a plague lesion on his thigh—and a
dog that's licking it.

Reason: According to legend, St. Rocco could cure plague victims
by making the sign of the cross over their bodies. Even so, he eventually caught the disease himself. Too selfless to seek treatment
(and apparently incapable of curing his own case), he went out into
the woods to die so that someone else could have his hospital bed.
A dog who found him there licked his lesions clean and began
bringing him food—and a few days later brought his master to the
site. The man nursed Rocco back to health, and he went back to
work helping plague victims.

Note: Rocco spent his spare time curing cattle of *their* diseases; for
this reason he is the patron saint of both plague sufferers *and* cattle.

SAINT GUIGNOLE (sixth century)

How He's Portrayed: With an erection.

Reason: He's the patron saint of impotence and infertility. One
church in the French city of Brest owns a wooden stature of the
saint whose most prominent feature, according to one source, is "a
rigidly protruding male member." Generations of the faithful have
whittled off slivers of the statue's manhood in the belief that the
chunks cured impotence, infertility, and other inadequacies. (Even
so, the statue's most famous attribute has remained completely
intact, a fact the locals attribute to divine intervention.)

SAINT CECILIA (date unknown)

How She's Portrayed: With three wounds in her throat.

Reason: According to a legend the Penguin *Dictionary of Saints* says "can only be regarded as a fabrication," Cecilia was a young woman who was condemned to suffocate in her own steam room after she refused to participate in a pagan ritual. When that didn't kill her, a soldier was sent in to chop off her head. He swung three times but failed to sever the head completely—and Roman law forbade a forth attempt—so Cecilia was left to linger in her bathtub, where she died from her wounds three days later.

SAINT LUCY OF SYRACUSE (304)

How She's Portrayed: Carrying her eyeballs on a platter.

Reason: Lucy was a pretty young Sicilian girl sworn to religious chastity—and was so determined to keep her vow that when a suitor complemented her on her beautiful eyes, she plucked them out and gave them to him. (They were later miraculously restored.) The man was so impressed he converted to Christianity.

SAINT FLORIAN (c. 304)

How He's Portrayed: Being thrown into a river with a stone tied around his neck.

Reason: A Roman army officer and closet Christian during the anti-Christian persecutions, Florian finally confessed his faith in 304 A.D. His superiors whipped him, skinned him alive, tied a millstone around his neck, and threw him into a river.

SAINT COSMAS AND SAINT DAMIAN (c. 303)

How They're Portrayed: Grafting the leg of a black man onto the body of a white man.

Reason: Known as "the moneyless ones" because they practiced medicine among the poor for free, Cosmas and Damian reportedly amputated the diseased leg of a white man and replaced it with the leg of a black man who had just died.

CATHOLIC CUISINE

The next time you munch on a pretzel, sip champagne, or quaff
a cappuccino, remember this: They were all discovered,
invented, or inspired by the Catholic Church.

COFFEE. Probably the only food discovered by a monk and officially approved by a pope. According to legend, coffee was discovered more than a thousand years ago when a friar in an Arabian convent noticed his goats prancing on their hind legs after eating berries from a wild coffee plant. He tried the beans himself; soon afterwards a new medicine was born.

Drinking coffee for the sheer pleasure of it didn't come until years later . . . and it didn't come without a fight: Sold in popular coffeehouses known as "penny universities" and "seminars of sedition," coffee was denounced by devout Christians as "the devil's brew" and outlawed by secular authorities, who saw it as an intoxicating beverage that led to "discussions of rebellion and slander of those in power." Church opposition finally ended in 1594, when Pope Clement VIII tried a cup and liked it so much that he baptized it. "We will not let coffee remain the property of Satan," he announced. "As Christians, our power is greater than Satan's; we shall make coffee our own." (Thank God.)

PRETZELS. Salted breads have been around for thousands of years—but it wasn't until about 610 A.D. that an Italian monk twisted them into their distinctive crisscross shape, which is supposed to look like two arms folded in prayer. The monk created these *pretioles*, or "little gifts," to give as a reward to children who memorized their prayers. By 1200 A.D. they were popular all over Europe.

McDONALD'S FILET-O-FISH SANDWICH. Remember meatless Fridays? They were the inspiration for McDonald's Filet-

When Pope Paul I died in 767, his brother Stephen II (III) was elected to replace him.

O-Fish sandwich, which was developed in 1962 by Louis Groen, owner of the burger chain's franchises in Cincinnati, Ohio. His restaurants made money every day except Friday, when the city's huge Catholic population skipped McDonald's in favor of competitors offering fish and other nonmeat entrees.

The sandwich was hardly a sure thing: When Groen first suggested it to McDonald's founder Ray Kroc, the fast food king snapped, "Hell, no! I don't care if the pope himself comes to Cincinnati. He can eat hamburgers like everybody else. We are not going to stink up our restaurants with any of your damned old fish!" Kroc preferred his own Hulaburger—pineapple and cheese on a bun—but that bombed, so he approved the fishburger, as he explained in his book, *Grinding It Out: The Making of McDonald's:*

> We started selling it only on Fridays in limited areas, but we got so many requests for it that in 1965 we made it available in all our stores every day, advertising it as the "fish that catches people." . . . I told [McDonald's executives], "You fellows just watch: Now that we've invested in all this equipment to handle fish, the Pope will change all the rules." A few years later, damned if he didn't.

Even so, the Filet-O-Fish is still a hit.

HOT CROSS BUNS. First baked by the pagan Saxons, who called them *bouns* (Saxon for "sacred ox"—and an ancestor of the word "bun") and baked them with X marks representing ox horns. The rolls were so popular that when the Christians began converting the Saxons to Christianity, rather than abolish the rolls they just rotated them forty-five degrees, reinterpreted the pagan X mark as a Christian *cross* . . . and passed them out during Mass to win converts.

CHAMPAGNE. Invented by accident when Dom Perignon, a seventeenth-century Benedictine monk from the Champagne region of France, began stuffing corks into the bottles of wine produced at his abbey. Unlike traditional cloth rag stoppers, which

The Book of Esther in the Old Testament does not mention God even once.

allowed carbon dioxide to escape, corks were airtight and caused bubbles to form. Amazingly, Dom Perignon thought the bubbles were a sign of poor quality—and devoted his entire life to *removing* them; but he never succeeded. Louis XIV took such a liking to champagne that he began drinking it exclusively; thanks to his patronage, by the 1700s champagne was a staple of French cuisine.

CAPPUCCINOS. Inspired by Matteo da Bascio, a sixteenth-century Franciscan monk living in Italy. In 1525 he founded the Capuchins, an offshoot reform movement within the Franciscan order whose members walked barefoot, wore long beards, and led lives of poverty and isolation. They also wore a brown, pointed hood (called *cappuccino* in Italian) like the one Saint Francis wore. Cappuccinos—a drink made with thick coffee and lots of foamy milk—get their name because they are roughly the same color as the hoods the Capuchins wore.

NUN'S FARTS. According to legend, hundreds of years ago a young nun farted while cooking a meal at the Abbey of Marmoutier in France. Some other nuns heard the fart and burst out laughing; and the young nun was so embarrassed that she dropped a ball of dough into a pot of boiling oil . . . where it immediately expanded into a fluffy golden nugget. Another nun fished it out and ate it; it tasted so good that the nuns prepared all of the dough that way. The little doughnuts—christened *pet de nonnes*, or "nun's farts"—became so popular that the Old English word *farte* became synonymous with balls of light pastry.

. . . FOOD FOR THOUGHT
Oliver Cromwell was a seventeenth-century Puritan dictator of England who brutally oppressed the Roman Catholics in his realm, including priests and nuns. He was a jerk at the dinner table too—here's the prayer he frequently said as grace:
"Some people have food, but no appetite; some people have an appetite, but no food. I have both. The Lord be praised!"

There are 27 chapels, 48 altars . . . and 800 chandeliers in St. Peter's Basilica.

CHURCH LINGO

*Here are some of the more unusual words and phrases
used by Catholics. Recognize any of them?*

Abba: A New Testament word that means "father" in Aramaic.

Gyrovagi: Wandering monks who either don't belong to a monastery or don't live in the one they do belong to.

Sexagesima: The second Sunday before Lent.

Stoup: A vessel that contains holy water.

Hebdomadarius: The person assigned by a religious community to lead daily prayers for the week.

Cubiculum: A burial chamber in a catacomb.

Ejaculation: A short prayer, like "My Jesus, mercy," or "My Lord and my God." Also known as an aspiration.

Mustum: Unfermented grape juice that alcoholic priests use to celebrate Mass.

Hair Shirt: A scratchy, coarse undergarment worn by Christian ascetics as a form of mortification and discipline.

Demoniac: A person possessed by a demon.

Energumen: Another word for a demoniac.

Leper Window: A low window, found in the walls of many medieval churches, through which lepers could observe and attend Mass.

Papabile: An informal name for a cardinal thought to be in the running to be elected the next pope.

Plumbator: The Vatican official who affixes the papal seal to important pontifical documents.

Protomartyr: The first cleric killed in a particular country because of his missionary work.

The Roman Catholic Church is larger than all other Christian sects combined.

OUR FATHER,
WHO ART IN PASTA...

They say the Lord works in mysterious ways. Don't believe it?
Take a look at some places he's been spotted recently . . .

THE SPAGHETTI CHRIST, Stone Mountain, Georgia

Background: In May 1991 Joyce Simpson, an Atlanta fashion
designer, was pulling out of the Stone Mountain Texaco station
when something unusual caught her eye. "I looked up and saw
Christ's face in a Pizza Hut sign," she said later, claiming the face
was visible in a forkful of spaghetti shown in the billboard. (She
also claims that at the very moment she saw the image, she was
considering dropping out of her church choir to begin a profes-
sional singing career.)

What happened: She stuck with the choir.

Update: About a dozen people dropped by the Texaco station to
look at the sign . . . but not everyone saw Jesus. Some saw dead
rock star Jim Morrison; others saw Willie Nelson. Most people just
saw spaghetti. What did Pizza Hut have to say about the incident?
"I think it's like looking at clouds," a company spokesman told
reporters. "Nobody's right, nobody's wrong. There's no intent on
our part to do anything subliminal."

THE MARBLE PILLAR JESUS, Hamilton County, Ohio

Background: In September 1993 municipal court judge Leslie Isa-
iah Gaines was trudging up the stairs of the Hamilton County
courthouse when he saw the face of Jesus in the swirls of a marble
column near the stairs on the second floor. (Gaines, who according to press reports was fifty pounds overweight and suffering from
high blood pressure at the time, denies that fatigue brought on by
the stair climb contributed to the apparition.) "Some might joke
about this," he said of the sighting, "but I turned the corner and

Pentecost means "fiftieth" in Greek; it falls 50 days after Jesus' crucifixion.

saw his face. I saw his crown of thorns, a bloodstained eye, his beard, the look of sorrow on his face. I felt I got a wake-up call from God."

What Happened: Gaines kept the sighting a secret for more than five months . . . and then went public in a letter he wrote to reporters. Why wait so long? He didn't want his colleagues to think he was crazy. "To tell lawyers and judges that I saw the face of Jesus in the courthouse would be like telling them that I had seen a UFO," he admits. At last report, he still sees the face of Jesus every day.

THE TORTILLA CHRIST, Lake Arthur, New Mexico

Background: On October 5, 1977, Maria Rubio was rolling her husband a burrito. "On the last roll," she later told a reporter, "I noticed something that looked like a face"—and immediately recognized it as the face of Jesus.

What Happened: She saved the tortilla, framed it, and built a shrine for it in her living room. Skeptics have suggested that the three- by- three- inch "unusual-looking, brown, singed spot" is nothing more than random burn marks from the skillet, but Rubio's faith remains unshaken. (One reporter even suggested the image looked more like boxer Leon Spinks . . . but was unable to provide a rational explanation why God would burn *his* face into a tortilla.)

Update: By 1987 more than eleven thousand people had visited the shrine.

THE REFRIGERATOR JESUS, Estill Springs, Tennessee

Background: In 1987 Arlene Gardner bought a new refrigerator and dragged her old one out onto the front porch of her trailer. A few nights later she noticed several of her neighbors outside staring at the old fridge. They told her that an image of Jesus had appeared on its side. Gardner took a look and saw it too—a "bearded profile" that she felt must surely be the Lord.

17

What Happened: Word of the miracle quickly spread; within days more than two thousand people a night were driving past Gardner's trailer to see Christ for themselves . . . until her neighbors discovered that their porch light caused the image when it reflected off the side of the fridge. (They disconnected the light . . . and the image went away.) Gardner remains convinced that Jesus really *did* make an appearance; others are not so sure. As one local skeptic put it, "When the good Lord comes, he won't come on a major appliance."

JESUS ON A SOYBEAN OIL TANK, Fostoria, Ohio

Background: Rita Ratchen was driving home from work one night in July 1986 when she saw the images of Jesus and a small child on the side of a storage tank containing soybean oil. "I wouldn't have wanted to tell everybody about it—I didn't want to be considered a kook," she said afterwards, admitting that she only went public after other people reported seeing the same thing.

What Happened: Hundreds of the faithful and merely curious drove to the site each night, causing traffic jams more than four miles long. . . . But things didn't really get crazy until a few weeks later, when someone noticed *another* image of Christ—this time just his face—on the other side of the tank. Archer Daniels Midland, the tank's owner, dismissed the apparitions as the combination of rust, paint, and shadows illuminated by some nearby spotlights and said that the images appeared shortly after some repairs were made on the tank. But the faithful kept coming . . . until the company painted over the tank and the images disappeared. Still, Ratchen and others pooh-pooh the notion that images are anything other than supernatural. "It's sad," she later observed, "that an image has to appear on a tank to make us think, when he is in church all the time."

POPE-O-CIDE

You know that Pope John Paul II was almost assassinated in 1981—but did you know that as many as 40 other popes may have been murdered? Here are some of their stories.

POPE SAINT CLEMENT I (c. 91-c. 101)
Cause of Death: According to legend, Roman officials tied an anchor around his neck and threw him into a river; because of this, he is usually depicted in art next to an anchor. (The *Oxford Dictionary of Popes* says the legend is "without foundation.")

POPE CALLISTUS I (217-222)
Cause of Death: According to legend, he was thrown down a well; but official sources say he was murdered by a rioting mob.

POPE SAINT PONTIAN (230-235)
Cause of Death: Starvation.
The Story: Pontian was arrested and deported to Sardinia (known then as the "island of death" due to its harsh conditions) during the persecutions of the Roman Emperor Maximinus Thrax. He died from exposure and harsh treatment not long after his arrival.
Historical Note: Saint Pontian abdicated the papal throne before he was arrested, the first pope in history to abdicate.

POPE SIXTUS II (257-258)
Cause of Death: Arrested and beheaded during the persecutions of the Roman emperor Valerian.

POPE JOHN VIII (872-882)
Cause of Death: Poisoned by member of his entourage and clubbed to death with a hammer.
The Story: Four years into his papacy, John made enemies in the

Babe Ruth was Catholic. So were Yogi Berra and Knute Rockne.

church by excommunicating powerful bishops and other officials he believed were plotting to overthrow him. They struck back in 882. According to one account, the plotters convinced one of John's relatives to serve him a poisoned drink . . . but it didn't kill him quickly enough, so they beat him to death instead.

POPE MARTIN I (649-653)

Cause of Death: Starved in exile.

The Story: An ailing but fiercely independent pontiff, Martin was elected pope without the permission of Roman emperor Constans II, who traditionally had the right to approve candidates for the papacy. This alone would have gotten him into trouble, and he made matters even worse by publicly condemning the emperor as a heretic and ordering him to repent. The rebuke so outraged Constans that he had the bedridden pope arrested, brought to Constantinople, and placed in solitary confinement. (During the trip the already ailing pope came down with dysentery and a severe case of gout.) Three months later the pope was tried for treason, found guilty, and sentenced to death. But instead of carrying out the sentence, Constans had Martin exiled to the Crimea, where he died of malnutrition and related causes eighteen months later.

POPE JOHN XII (955-964)

Cause of Death: Beaten to death while committing adultery.

The Story: A notorious womanizer, Pope John was violating the sixth and ninth commandments with a married woman when her husband walked in and caught them in the act. The husband beat John severely; he died of his injuries a few days later. (According to another version of the story, John died of a *stroke* while committing adultery.) He was twenty-seven.

POPE BENEDICT VI (973-974)

Cause of Death: Strangled in prison.

The Story: An unpopular candidate for the papacy, Benedict got

Pope John Paul II is the first non-Italian pontiff since Adrian IV (1522-1523).

the job only because he had been handpicked by the Holy Roman Emperor, Otto I. But when the emperor died a few months later, the powerful families of Rome dumped the new pope in favor of their own candidate, Boniface VII. Boniface had Benedict thrown into prison—and when it appeared that the *new* emperor, Otto II, was going to restore him to the papacy, he had Benedict strangled. But the murder so outraged the Roman populace that Boniface had to flee to Constantinople, where he spent the next eight years plotting his return to Rome (see below).

POPE JOHN XIV (983-984)

Cause of Death: Starved in prison.

The Story: The circumstances surrounding Benedict VI's murder repeated themselves in 983, when Emperor Otto II died within days of naming an unpopular bishop, John XIV, as pope. When Boniface VII—still in exile in Constantinople—learned of the emperor's death, he returned to Rome, deposed Pope John, and locked him up in prison, where he starved to death four months later. Boniface remained pope until July 20, 985, when he died of sudden and unexplained causes. (He was still *very* unpopular—when the Roman citizens learned of his death, they seized his body, stripped it of its papal robes, and dragged it naked through the streets to the front of the papal palace . . . where they trampled it and stabbed it with spears.)

. . . ONE THAT GOT AWAY

"Not all plots succeeded," says John Cornwell in his book *A Thief in the Night: The Mysterious Death of Pope John Paul I*. In the sixteenth century, he writes, "a Florentine surgeon was hired by five cardinals to murder [Pope Leo X] by introducing poison into his anal passage while pretending to treat his holiness' piles [hemorrhoids]. The conspiracy was discovered and the ringleader, Cardinal Alfonso Petrucci, was strangled with a rope of crimson silk." Pope Leo died in 1521 at the age of forty-five. Cause of death: most likely, malaria.

According to official church estimates, at least 40 popes bribed their way into office.

THE SLOW MARTYRS

Is sanity a requirement for sainthood? You would think so . . .
but the people listed below might make you wonder.

FOR MARTYRS ONLY
In the earliest days of the Catholic Church, it was easy to decide who qualified for sainthood and who didn't: If you had been *martyred* (killed for your religious beliefs), you were a saint—and if you hadn't, you weren't. It was that simple. Why? Because in its earliest form the veneration of saints consisted simply of the survivors of persecutions honoring the memory of their fallen comrades. Each church kept a list of the important martyrs in the area, and on the anniversary of their death it celebrated Mass at their tomb. If you weren't a martyr, there wasn't any reason to put you on the list.

The Right Stuff. But as the persecutions wound down at the end of the third century, an inevitable question arose: How could a Christian who *hadn't* been persecuted achieve sainthood? Today the answer is clear: You have to lead a holy life. But in the fourth century the solution wasn't so simple, and the early Christians—with the crucifixion and their own just-ended persecutions so strongly etched in their memory—came to a different conclusion: It wasn't whether you *lived* as Christ had; it was whether you had *suffered* as he had that proved you were a saint. And since the Romans were no longer inflicting suffering on the Christians, the Christians began inflicting it on *themselves*.

THE ASCETICS
A new category of saint was born: the "slow martyr" or *ascetic*. By denying himself the pleasures of the world—which in many cases included food, clothing, shelter, sleep . . . and hygiene—the ascetic "confessed" his faith to God and man alike. "To the Church," says Ken Woodward in his book *Making Saints*, "the slow

In 1714 the Catholic Church forbade adulterers from naming their lovers during 'white martyrdom' of the ascetics was the virtual equivalent of the immediate 'red' martyrdom of those who had actually shed their blood. In short, to the question 'Who is a saint?' the Christians of Greco-Roman antiquity responded by pointing to examples of exceptional suffering."

Most of the ascetics practiced relatively mild forms of austerity such as shunning material possessions or fasting periodically. But others were downright bizarre. Some examples:

SAINT ANTONY THE GREAT (251-356).

Antony was only eighteen when his parents died in 269 and left him guardian of his younger sister. Determined to do what was right, he dumped his sister in a convent, distributed his parents' entire estate to the poor (including his sister's share), and then struck out on his own peculiar path to holiness. First stop: an abandoned tomb in an old cemetery outside of town, where he lived as a hermit for more than thirteen years. He fought constantly with the devil (who appeared to him in "terrifying forms," among them "a beautiful naked woman" and "a Negro") —and ate only one bread-and-water meal a day. Is cleanliness next to godliness? Not as far as Antony was concerned: According to his friend and biographer Saint Athanasius, he "neither bathed his body with water to free himself from filth, nor did he ever wash his feet, nor even endure so much as to put them into water, unless compelled by necessity."

Word of Antony's lifestyle spread over time, and the tomb where he lived attracted throngs of admirers who, though well behaved, were extremely distracting. So in 292 he moved to an old fort atop a nearby mountain where, "eating only what was thrown to him over the wall of the fort," he again found solitude . . . for a while. By 305 the mountaintop was literally crawling with groupies; so much so that Antony organized them into a structured community—the world's first Christian monastery. He eventually retired to a cave on a mountaintop, where he died at the age of 105.

confession. Why? It learned that priests "were making carnal use of the information."

SAINT HILARION (291-371). One of Antony's original groupies, Hilarion committed to the ascetic life after a visit to the famous saint and lived in a tiny hut in the middle of the Gaza desert. His diet consisted of fifteen figs per day, "eaten at sunset."

SAINT PAUL THE HERMIT. For more than ninety years Paul lived in a cave in the desert and wore nothing but leaves he took from a nearby palm tree. Like Hilarion, he lived largely on figs, but according to legend his diet was supplemented by "half a loaf of bread that a raven brought him each day." Saint Antony visited him in his old age and lived with him until he died. After Antony moved in, the legend assures us, "the raven brought, every day, a *whole* loaf of bread." (He is sometimes called Paul the *First* Hermit "to distinguish him from other hermits named Paul.")

SAINT MARY MAGDALENE DEI PAZZI (1556-1607). One of the most unusual nuns in Catholic history, Saint Mary regularly ran through the grounds of her convent whipping herself and rolling in thorn bushes. (She often begged the other nuns to tie her up and splash her with hot wax, but they seldom obliged.) She also regularly experienced ecstasies—which today might be known as bouts of madness. In recognition of her passion for suffering, she is usually painted with her breasts on fire.

SAINT ROSE OF LIMA (1586-1671). Rose was a Dominican *tertiary* (affiliated with a convent but not a full nun) living in Lima, Peru, in the sixteenth century. She lived in a hut in her parents' garden, wore a crown of thorns, and slept on a bed of broken glass. She often dragged a heavy cross behind her when she went for walks and on other occasions whipped herself with chains. Disgusted with her considerable physical beauty, she also rubbed hot peppers into her cheeks, smeared her hands and lips with caustic quicklime, and dug out chunks of her skin with broken glass. Friends and loved ones foolishly thought her insane—but the faithful recognized her holiness, and her garden hut eventually became the spiritual center of Lima.

Clerical dress rule: Only popes are allowed to wear velvet.

MODERN-DAY LATIN

Did you know that the Vatican still conducts its official business in Latin? That doesn't sound like a big deal, but it is: Few if any modern topics can be discussed in a language that's been dead for centuries. How does the Vatican handle this problem? Every thirty years or so, it makes up new words—and publishes them in a special dictionary called the Lexicon Recentis Latinitatis. Here are some selections from the 1991 edition:

amnesia: *memoriae amissio*

baby sitter: *infantaria*

bidet: *ovata pelvis*

bottle washer: *machina lagoenis expurgandis*

brainwash: *coercitio mentis*

car wash: *aeris benzinique mixtura*

cellulite: *cellutis*

Christmas tree: *arbor natalicia*

cover girl: *exterioris paginae puella*

disc brakes: *sufflamen disci forma*

discotheque: *orbium phonographicorum theca*

fax: *exemplum simillime expressum*

flamenco: *Vandaliciana saltatio*

flashbulb: *fulgor photographicus*

to flirt: *lusorie amare*

guerrilla warfare: *bellum tectum*

gulag (Soviet prison camp): *campus captivis custodiendis*

photocopy: *exemplar luce expressum*

pinball machine: *sphaeriludium electricum nomismate actum*

refrigerator: *cella frigorifera*

secret agent: *speculator tectus*

to be lazy at work: *neglenter operari*

television: *instrumentum televisificum*

traffic jam: *fluxus interclusio*

travel agency: *itinerum procuratio*

warmonger: *belli instigator*

washing machine: *machina linteorum lavatoria*

Eighty-seven percent of priests, and 88% of nuns, say they're happy in their vocations.

COUNT DRACULA: THE CATHOLIC CONNECTION

You probably know that Bram Stoker's Dracula *was inspired by Vlad ("the Impaler") Dracula, a real-life fifteenth-century Romanian tyrant. Here are some things you didn't know about him:*

The name "Dracula" comes from a Catholic honor society. In 1431 the Holy Roman Emperor Sigismund invested Vlad's father, who was also named Vlad, in the Order of the Dragon, a secret fraternity of Catholic knights sworn to defend Christendom against the Ottoman Turks. The elder Vlad painted a big green dragon on his shield in honor of his new knighthood, and when he became prince of Walachia (part of modern-day Romania) in 1437, his subjects nicknamed him *Dracul*, Romanian for "the dragon." Vlad Jr. took the name *Dracula*, "son of the dragon."

Note: It was Dracula's *name*, not his terrible deeds, that first made him the living embodiment of evil. To this day the word *dracul* can be translated as either "the dragon" *or* "the devil" in Romanian—the concepts are interchangeable—and when the elder Dracul returned from Nuremberg with the big dragon on his shield, his subjects took it to mean that he had literally joined forces with the devil.

Dracula was probably baptized a Catholic. The Dracul family was Roman Catholic when Dracula was born in 1431, and many historians speculate he was baptized into the Catholic faith. But when Dracul became prince of Walachia six years later, he was required to convert to the Romanian Orthodox Church; and the rest of the family made the switch with him. Dracula remained a Romanian Orthodox until 1476, when he converted back to Catholicism.

He wore his trademark black cape for religious reasons. Knights of the Order of the Dragon wore green capes—except on Fridays and holy days honoring the crucifixion, when they wore the traditional black cape of mourning. No word on whether Bram Stoker's Dracula wore *his* black cape for religious purposes . . . but the original Dracula did.

He earned the nickname "the Impaler" fighting for the pope. Dracula was a butcher even by medieval standards: Though he ruled a country of only five hundred thousand citizens, during his lifetime Dracula managed to murder an estimated one hundred thousand people using the cruelest tortures he could think of, as the papal ambassador reported to Pope Pius II in 1462:

> He killed some of them by breaking them under the wheels of carts; others, stripped of their clothes, were skinned alive up to their entrails . . . others punctured with stakes piercing their head, their navel, breast, and what is even unworthy of relating, their buttocks and the middle of their entrails, and emerging from their mouths . . . he killed others in other ferocious ways, torturing them with varied instruments such as the atrocious cruelties of the most frightful tyrants could devise.

. . . But he didn't earn the nickname *Kaziklu Bey* ("the Impaler") until 1462, when Pope Pius II called for a crusade against Turks and the rulers of Europe ignored him . . . except for Dracula, who threw twenty to thirty thousand Walachian men, women, and children into battle against the Ottoman sultan Mohammed II and his 250,000-man army. Amazingly, Dracula won—not through superior numbers or superior fighting, but through superior butchery: When the sultan marched on the Walachian capital of Tirgoviste in June of 1462, Dracula repelled the attack by impaling more than twenty thousand captured Turkish soldiers on pikes along a mile-long stretch of road leading to the city, a scene that became known as "the forest of the impaled." According to Ray McNally, author of several books on Dracula, "The sultan looked and said, 'Is it worth it?' His troops were frightened and they turned back."

father children). His wife and daughter lived with him in the papal palace.

HOLY ORDERS

Here's a look at the Rule of St. Benedict, *one of the most influential documents in Catholic Church history. Convents and monasteries have followed its guidelines for more than 1,450 years.*

WORDS TO LIVE BY
In 529 A.D., Saint Benedict of Nursia gathered his disciples together and founded a monastery at Monte Cassino in Italy. To maintain order among his "Benedictines," he wrote the *Rule*, a strict list of regulations for them to live by. It proved so timeless and effective that many monastic orders still follow its guidelines today.

. . . But not all of the regulations have survived the test of time. Take these rules, for example:

"The monastery should be planned, if possible, with all the necessities—water, mill, garden, shops—within the walls. Thus the monks will not need to wander about outside, for this is not good for their souls."

✠ ✠ ✠

"A wise old monk should guard the gates of the monastery. He shall know how to receive and answer a question, and be old enough so he will not be able to wander far."

✠ ✠ ✠

"Anyone who leaves the monastery, goes anywhere, or does anything, however small, without the abbot's permission will be [punished]. . . . No one shall recount his adventures outside the monastery, because this is most harmful. Violators will be subject to regular punishment."

✠ ✠ ✠

"The sick should be permitted baths as often as necessary, but the healthy and especially the young are to bathe rarely."

The Bible doesn't say what kind of fruit got Adam and Eve kicked out of the

"All the monks shall sleep in separate beds. . . . The younger brothers should not [sleep] next to one another. Rather their beds should be interspersed with those of their elders. . . . [All monks] will sleep in their robes, belted but with no knives, thus preventing injury in slumber."

✠ ✠ ✠

"No matter how perfect the disciple, nor how good and pious his speech, he rarely should be given permission to speak. . . . We always condemn and ban all small talk and jokes; no disciple shall speak such things."

✠ ✠ ✠

"Under no circumstances should complaining be tolerated, no matter what the reason. Anyone found complaining should be subjected to the most severe punishment."

✠ ✠ ✠

"If one makes a mistake in chanting a psalm, responsory antiphon, or in reading a lesson, he must immediately humble himself publicly. . . . Children should be whipped for such mistakes."

✠ ✠ ✠

"Youths who are at fault, or those who cannot understand the gravity of excommunication, shall receive just punishment (enforced fasting or flogging) so that they may be healed."

✠ ✠ ✠

"If a brother does not change his evil ways, despite correction, even excommunication [exclusion from normal monastic life], then he must be punished more severely—for example, by whipping. . . . If even this has no effect, let [the Abbot] try greater things. . . ."

Garden of Eden, but most biblical scholars agree that it probably *wasn't* an apple.

THE AWFUL DISCLOSURES OF MARIA MONK

Here's the inside story on what one scholar has called "by far the most influential single work of American nativist propaganda in the period preceding the Civil War."

AN UNCONVENTIONAL CONVENT
Have you heard of the Hôtel-Dieu convent in Montreal, Canada? This infamous nineteenth-century nunnery was connected to a nearby monastery by a secret underground tunnel, which enabled priests and nuns to travel back and forth whenever they wanted and throw wild orgies completely unnoticed by the outside world. Birth control wasn't a problem: Whenever a nun got pregnant, the other nuns strangled the newborn (after *baptizing* it, of course, so that it would go straight to heaven) and threw it into a huge lime-filled pit dug in the cellar for that purpose; any nun that protested was also murdered and thrown into the pit. The scandal went on for decades, until a nun named Maria Monk escaped and told her story to the world.

Does this story sound preposterous? It *is*. There was an Hôtel-Dieu nunnery in Montreal in the nineteenth century; it was one of the oldest and most respected Catholic institutions in Canada. But there was no tunnel, there were no orgies, and there was no lime pit in the cellar filled with baby corpses. The whole story was a lie—but it was one of the most widely believed anti-Catholic lies of the nineteenth and twentieth centuries. It's mostly forgotten now, but if you grew up in the 1960s or earlier, your Protestant schoolmates may have taunted you with tales of sex-crazed, baby-killing nuns and unmarked graves, unearthed at convents, that were teeming with the tiny skeletons of murdered infants.

SISTER ACT
The entire story was the result of one book: *The Awful Disclosures*

According to an ancient scroll unearthed in Japan in 1988, Jesus married a woman

of Maria Monk, which was published in 1836 by Monk, an unwed mother claiming to be an escapee from the nunnery, and the Reverend J. J. Slocum, a fiery Protestant preacher and anti-Catholic bigot. *Awful Disclosures* couldn't have come at a worse time: Anti-Catholic hysteria was sweeping the country, brought on by the large number of Catholic immigrants entering the U.S. from the 1820s onward. The country's first "no popery" newspaper opened for business in 1830, and in 1834 an Ursuline convent in Charleston, Massachusetts, was burned to the ground by an angry mob. When *The Awful Disclosures of Maria Monk* hit the shelves in 1836, it was an instant best-seller and sold more than three hundred thousand copies by the start of the Civil War.

LIFE AT THE HÔTEL-DIEU

It's hard to understand how so many people could be fooled by such an outlandish story—until you actually read it yourself. Written in the form of an autobiography, The Awful Disclosures of Maria Monk *is surprisingly convincing. If you had been living in the 1830s, didn't know much about life in a nunnery . . . and didn't particularly like Catholics, you might have been fooled by it, too. See for yourself:*

THE TUNNEL OF LOVE

"I was passing one day through a part of the convent cellar, where I had not often occasion to go, when the toe of my shoe hit something. I tripped and fell down. I rose again, and holding my lamp to see what had caused my fall, I found an iron ring, fastened to a small square trapdoor. This I had the curiosity to raise, and saw four or five steps leading down, but there was not light enough to see more, and I feared to be noticed by somebody and reported to the Superior; so closing the door again, I left the spot. At first, I could not imagine the use for such a passage; but it afterward occurred to me, that this might open to the subterranean passage to the Seminary, for I never before could account for the appearance of many of the priests, who often appeared and disappeared among us, particularly at night, when I knew the gates were

closed. They could, as I now saw, come up to the door of the
Superior's room at any hour, then up the stairs into our sleeping-
room, or where they chose. And often they were in our beds
before us. . . ."

A DARK SECRET

"The Mother Superior now informed me that, having taken the
black veil . . . I was now to have access to every part of the edifice.
. . . She gave me another piece of information which excited other
feelings in me, scarcely less dreadful. Infants were sometimes born
in the convent, but they were always baptized and immediately
strangled! This secured their everlasting happiness; for the baptism purified them from all sinfulness, and being sent out of the
world before they had time to do anything wrong, they were at
once admitted into heaven.

"How happy, she exclaimed, are those who secure immortal
happiness to such little beings! Their souls would thank those who
kill their bodies, if they had it in their power! Into what a place
and among what society had I been admitted! How differently did
a Convent now appear from what I had supposed it to be!"

DISCOVERING THE PIT

"Three or four days after my reception the Superior sent me in to
the cellar for coal; and after she had given me directions, I proceeded down a staircase, with a lamp in my hand. I soon found
myself upon the bare earth, in a spacious place, so dark, that I
could not at once distinguish its form, or size, but I observed that
it had very solid stone walls, and was arched overhead, at no great
elevation. Following my directions, I proceeded onwards from the
foot of the stairs, where appeared to be one end of the cellar. . . .

"Here the earth appeared as if mixed with some whitish substance, which attracted my attention. As I proceeded, I found the
whiteness increase, until the surface looked almost like snow, and
in a short time I observed before me, a hole dug so deep into the
earth that I could perceive no bottom. I stopped to observe it—it

The American Bible Society has distributed more than a billion Bibles since 1816.

was circular, perhaps twelve or fifteen feet across; in the middle of the cellar, and unprotected by any kind of curb, so that one might easily have walked into it.

"The white substance was spread all over the surface around it; and lay in such quantity on all sides, that it seemed as if a great deal of it must have been thrown into the hole. It immediately occurred to me that the white substance was lime, and that this must be the place where the infants were buried, after being murdered, as the Superior had informed me. . . .

"I passed the spot, therefore, with distressing thoughts, it is true, about the little corpses, which might be in that secret burying place, but with recollections also of the declarations which I had heard, about the favor done their souls by sending them straight to heaven. . . ."

BABY KILLING

"I was one day in the nuns' private sick-room, when I had an opportunity, unsought for, of witnessing deeds of such a nature. Two little twin babes, the children of [Sister] Sainte Catherine, were brought to a priest, who was in the room for baptism. I was present while the ceremony was performed, with the Superior and several of the old nuns, whose names I never knew. . . .

"The priest then on duty was Father Larkin. He is a good-looking European, and has a brother who is a professor of the college. He first put oil upon the heads of the infants, as is the custom before baptism. When he had baptized the children, they were taken, one after another, by one of the old nuns, in the presence of us all. She pressed her hand upon the mouth and nose of the first, so tight that it could not breathe, and in a few minutes, when the hand was removed, it was dead. She then took the other, and treated it in the same way. No sound was heard, and both the children were corpses. The greatest indifference was shown by all present during this operation; for all, as I well know, were long accustomed to such scenes. The little bodies were then taken to the cellar, thrown into the pit, and covered with a quantity of lime.

33

"That others were killed in the same manner during my stay in the nunnery, I am well assured. How many there were I cannot tell, and having taken no account of those I heard of, I cannot speak with precision; I believe, however, that I learnt through nuns, that at least eighteen or twenty infants were smothered, and secretly buried in the cellar, while I was a nun."

WHAT HAPPENED

When the book first appeared in January 1836, the public didn't quite know what to make of it. The Catholic press immediately denounced it as a falsehood, and most Protestant papers were cautious at first—although they agreed that the scenes of nunnery life it depicted were "typical of all convents"—but they eventually came out in full support of the story. The Hôtel-Dieu refused to respond to the allegations, which only fueled suspicions.

Left to stand on its own merits, *The Awful Disclosures of Maria Monk* might well have collapsed under the weight of its outlandish claims—but with the religious newspapers vouching for its accuracy, the controversy continued to grow and the weight of public opinion turned strongly against the convent. The pressure on the Hôtel-Dieu was so great that in 1837 it broke its silence, denied the charges, and allowed two impartial Protestant clergymen into the convent to investigate whether the charges were true. Walking room by room through the entire nunnery, the preachers quickly arrived at two conclusions: There was no evidence to suggest that any of the activities Monk described had ever taken place; and that the Hôtel-Dieu convent in no way resembled the nunnery she had described in her book.

Did the on-site inspections prove that the allegations were false? Not at all—at least according to Reverend Slocum and Maria Monk. They charged that the Protestant clergymen who made the inspections were "Jesuits in disguise" and that masons and carpenters had rebuilt the innards of the entire convent to hide the evidence that the crimes had taken place.

The U.S. Catholic Church granted 16 annulments on grounds of impotence in 1990.

SISTER ACT II

To make matters worse, soon after the inspection another "nun," who called herself Sister Frances Patrick, came forward claiming that she had just escaped from the Hôtel-Dieu herself. She told reporters that workers had indeed rebuilt the convent—and that she had been present when the Protestant clergymen made their investigation. Furthermore, she alleged, the bodies of two dead babies were hidden in one of the closets during the inspection but that the clergymen had walked past the closet without looking inside it.

Sister Francis Patrick was quickly exposed as a fraud—but doubts about the Hôtel-Dieu continued to persist, so in 1837 the convent permitted Col. William L. Stone, editor of the respected New York *Commercial Advertiser*, to make a second inspection. Reading through a copy of *Awful Disclosures* as he went, Col. Stone spent almost an entire day touring the convent, "poking into every closet, climbing to a high window to see into an unopened room and smelling a row of jars in the basement which might have contained lime used in the disposal of infant's bodies," as he went. He literally searched every inch of the building and afterwards he announced, "I most solemnly believe that the priests and nuns are innocent in this matter."

Col. Stone's findings were devastating to Monk's credibility, and the Protestant papers began to turn against her. In June 1837 the *Christian Spectator* wrote, "If the natural history of 'gullibility' is ever written, the impostures of Maria Monk must hold a prominent place in its pages."

MORE SETBACKS

Is there any chance at all that Maria Monk's charges were true? Not really—that possibility evaporated in 1837, when reporters finally tracked down Maria's mother and got her side of the story, which the *Catholic Historical Review* later recounted:

> The account of Maria Monk's life given by her mother varied greatly from that contained in the *Awful Disclosures*. The

mother, a Protestant living near Montreal, testified that her daughter had never been in the Hôtel-Dieu convent and that the whole tale was the product of a brain injured in infancy when the child had run a slate pencil into her head. Maria Monk, the mother insisted, had been a wild girl who was constantly in trouble and had of necessity been confined in a Catholic Magdalen asylum in Montreal. Even there she had gotten into trouble and had been aided in her escape by a former lover, who was really the father of the child born in New York. In all probability, the mother's story was substantially correct.

As if the revelation that Monk had spent time in a Catholic *insane asylum*, not a convent, wasn't bad enough, in 1838 she gave birth to a second illegitimate child, and this time did not even bother to claim that it had been fathered by a priest. That wouldn't be such a big deal in the 1990s—but in the 1830s it destroyed her reputation in the eyes of pious Christian Protestants, the very people who had believed her charges in the first place. (One newspaper, the *American Protestant Vindicator*, continued to support her—it charged that the second pregnancy had been "arranged by Jesuits" to discredit her.)

THE END
Maria's career as an ex-nun was finished. She began a rapid descent into poverty and obscurity, eventually ending up as a call girl in a New York city brothel. But she was as dishonest a prostitute as she had been an ex-nun—and in 1849 was arrested for picking the pocket of one of her customers. She was imprisoned in New York's Welfare Island, where she died a few months later. Her book is still in print.

RECOMMENDED READING
The Awful Disclosures of Maria Monk, by Maria Monk (Manchester, N. H.: Ayer Press, 1977)

Famous forgotten date: March 18, 1966, the last day that getting married by

CATHOLIC
WORD ORIGINS

You probably don't realize it, but a lot of words we use in every-day speech have Roman Catholic origins. Some examples:

CHAPEL

Meaning: A private church.

Background: When Saint Martin of Tours died in the fourth century, his admirers kept his cape—called a *capella* in Latin—and built a shrine for it. The French named the shrine the *chapelle*, and when the English borrowed the word, they dropped the "le" and applied the word to any small place of worship . . . whether or not it had a cape in it.

Note: The person assigned to guard Saint Martin's cape was known as the *cappellanus* . . . which is the direct precursor of the English word "chaplain."

CONCLAVE

Meaning: An important or secret meeting.

Background: The word was born after Pope Clement IV died in 1268. It took so long to choose a successor that the local magistrates finally locked the College of Cardinals into an assembly hall *cum clave*—"with a key"—removed the roof, and fed them a starvation diet until they elected a new pope in 1271.

BONFIRE

Meaning: A large fire "specially built and lit to express public joy."

Background: A gruesome throwback to the reign of England's King Henry VIII, who had large fires specially built and lit to burn Catholics who refused to renounce the pope and accept him as the

a non-Catholic minister was grounds for excommunication.

leader of the English church. Originally spelled *bonefire*, the word gets its name from the fact that surviving Catholics plucked the bones of the dearly departed out of the ashes and preserved them as relics.

DECIMATE

Meaning: Today "decimate" means to destroy or kill a large part of something, but in the old days it was much more precise: It meant to kill every tenth person . . . and has the same root as "decimal" and "December."

Background: Decimation was the means by which the Roman military dealt with mutinous troops: It literally held a death lottery in which it killed one tenth of the rebellious soldiers by selecting names at random. One famous example was that of Saint Maurice and six hundred of his troops in approximately 287 A.D. When they refused to make sacrifices to pagan gods, one tenth of the soldiers were slaughtered. But they still refused to sacrifice, so another tenth were killed, and so on until everyone was dead—with Saint Maurice being the very last person martyred.

CEMETERY

Meaning: A place where the dead are buried.

Background: The word comes from *koimeterion*, the Greek word for "sleeping place." The early Christians were the first people to call graveyards cemeteries—they believed the bodies of the dead would be reunited with their souls on Judgment Day, which meant the corpse's placement in the cemetery was only temporary.

CATACOMB

Meaning: An underground burial vault.

Background: Yet another Catholic death innovation. The name came about by coincidence, thanks to the location of one of the early Christian grave sites on the Via Appia outside of Rome: It was *kata kumbas*—"near the low place"—between two hills.

Moses stuttered.

QUESTIONS AND ANSWERS: THE *BALTIMORE CATECHISM*

Remember the Baltimore Catechism? If you went to Catholic school in the 1970s or later, you've probably never heard of it. . . . If you went to Catholic school before the 1960s, you'll probably never forget it.

BACKGROUND. Who is God? Why can't we see him? Is it a sin to cut in line at the confessional? Catholic kids have pestered priests, nuns, and their parents with questions like these as long as the church has been around. They aren't always easy to answer—nor is it easy to teach kids basics of the faith without a lot of help. That's why the Church writes catechisms.

You might think of "catechism" as those after-school religion classes for public school kids, but in its most traditional form a catechism is a *booklet* of Christian doctrine. The most famous American version was the *Baltimore Catechism*, which was published in 1885 and used in Catholic schools until the early 1960s. In its heyday it was second only to the Bible in its influence on American Catholic life: Most Catholics over 40 know what they know about the basics of their faith because they read it in the *Baltimore Catechism*. The reforms of Vatican II have made it largely obsolete, but it's still fun to read. Here are some excerpts:

GOD: AN INTRODUCTION

Q. 132. Who is God?
A. God is the Creator of heaven and earth, and of all things.

Q. 166. Where is God?
A. God is everywhere.

Q. 167. How is God everywhere?
A. God is everywhere whole and entire as He is in any one place. This is true: We must believe it, though we cannot understand it.

Countries with the highest population density: Monaco, Singapore, and Vatican City.

Q. 168. If God is everywhere, why do we not see Him?
A. We do not see God, because He is a pure spirit and cannot be seen with bodily eyes.

THE SIGN OF THE CROSS

Q. 1064. How do we make the sign of the cross?
A. [Put] the right hand to the forehead, then on the breast, and then to the left and right shoulders, and say, "In the name of the Father, and of the Son, and of the Holy Ghost. Amen."

Q. 1065. What is a common fault we make blessing ourselves?
A. A common fault with many in blessing themselves is to make a hurried motion with the hand which is in no way a sign of the cross. They perform this act of devotion without thought or intention, forgetting that the Church grants an indulgence to all who bless themselves properly while they have sorrow for their sins.

ON CONFESSION

Q. 743. What faults do many commit preparing for confession?
A. In preparing for confession many commit the faults (1) of giving too much time to the examination of conscience and little or none in exciting themselves to true sorrow for the sins discovered; (2) of trying to recall every trifling circumstance, instead of thinking of the means by which they will avoid their sins for the future.

Q. 746. What faults are to be avoided in making confessions?
A. In making our confession we are to avoid (1) telling useless details, the sins of others, or the name of any person; (2) confessing sins we are not sure of having committed; exaggerating our sins or their number; multiplying the number of times a day by the number of days to get the exact number of habitual sins; (3) giving a vague answer, such as "sometimes," when asked how often; waiting after each sin to be asked for the next; (4) hesitating over sins through pretended modesty and thus delaying the priests and others; telling the exact words in each when we have committed sev-

Pope Adrian VI was so unpopular when he died in 1523 that the

eral sins of the same kind, cursing for example; and, lastly, leaving the confessional before the priest gives us a sign to go.

Q. 747. Is it wrong to go to confession out of turn?
A. It is wrong to go to confession out of turn against the will of others waiting with us, because (1) it causes disorder, quarreling and scandalous conduct in the Church; (2) it is unjust, makes others angry and lessens their good dispositions for confession; (3) it annoys and distracts the priest by the confusion and disorder it creates. It is better to wait than go to confession in an excited and disorderly manner.

ON THE FIFTH COMMANDMENT

Q. 1270. What is the fifth Commandment?
A. The fifth Commandment is: Thou shalt not kill.

Q. 1272. How do we know that this commandment forbids the killing only of human beings?
A. We know that this commandment forbids the killing only of human beings because, after giving this commandment, God commanded that animals be killed for sacrifice in the temple of Jerusalem, and God never contradicts Himself.

Q. 1276. Under what circumstances may human life be lawfully taken?
A. (1) in self-defense, when we are unjustly attacked and have no other means of saving our own lives; (2) in a just war, when the safety or rights of the nation require it; (3) by the lawful execution of a criminal, fairly tried and found guilty of a crime punishable by death when the preservation of law and order and the good of the community require such execution.

RECOMMENDED READING
The Baltimore Catechism #3 (Tan Books and Publishers, Inc., P.O. Box 424, Rockford, IL 61105).

citizens of Rome "adorned his doctor's house with flowers."

SHORT-LIVED POPES

Believe it or not, at least thirteen popes had shorter reigns than John Paul I (1978), who died only thirty-three days into his papacy. Here are some of their stories:

Pope **Stephen (II) (752).** Had a stroke three days after he was elected and died the next day, *before* he was consecrated pope. This raised a difficult question: Was an unconsecrated pontiff a true pope? For centuries the answer was no—and Stephen's name was kept off the official list of popes. But the church changed its mind in the 1500s and added him to the list. The only problem: Eight other popes had taken the name Stephen in the meantime, and inserting him in the list screwed up the numbering system (Stephen III was now Stephen IV, etc.). Papal scholars got around the confusion (some say they made it *worse*) by assigning dual numbers to all subsequent Pope Stephens: Stephen III is now Stephen III (IV), and so on.

Pope Urban VII (1590). Contracted malaria the day after his election and died twelve days later . . . before he could be consecrated. But since he lived in the sixteenth century, he didn't have any of the numerical woes that Stephen (II) did.

Pope Celestine IV (1241). When Pope Gregory IX died in 1241, the Roman senator Matteo Rosso Orsini tried to force the College of Cardinals to elect a candidate of his choosing. But they refused—so he locked them up in a dilapidated palace "in deliberately cruel and squalid conditions" until they picked a pope that met his approval. (Three cardinals died from the harsh treatment.) Sixty-six days later they elected Celestine IV as pope.

Celestine's most important qualification was his health, which wasn't good. In fact, he looked like he was about to die— which was precisely what the cardinals were looking for: Even

The religious tract *High-heeled Shoes for Dwarfs in Holiness*

after sixty-six days of negotiations they still couldn't agree on a candidate, but they wanted out of the palace—so they elected the sickest man they could think of, in the hope that he would die soon and they could elect another pope under freer circumstances. They got their wish—Celestine fell seriously ill two days later and died only seventeen days into his papacy. (It took the cardinals eighteen months to elect his successor.)

Pope Silvester III (1045). Became pope after Benedict IX, the previous pope, lost military control of the city and was deposed. But Benedict regained control twenty-two days later and gave his successor the boot. Demoted to bishop, Sylvester died in 1063.

Pope Benedict V (964). The middle of the tenth century was a time when the citizens of Rome struggled against the Holy Roman Emperor Otto I for control over who got to pick the pope. Otto won temporarily in 963 when he deposed Pope John XII and installed his own candidate, Leo VIII. But Leo fled Rome soon after Otto rejoined his army, and John XII reclaimed the throne.

When John XII died in May 964, Otto tried to reinstall Leo as pope . . . but the Roman citizens elected Benedict V instead, which made Otto so mad that he put Rome under seige. A month later the city surrendered: Benedict was hauled before Otto and Leo, demoted to deacon, and stripped of his papal robes; then Pope Leo beat him over the head with his pastoral staff. Benedict was exiled to Hamburg, where he died in July 966. His papacy lasted thirty-two days.

✠ ✠ ✠

. . . GONE TO POT:
Victoria, Seychelles: "Felix Paul, the Roman Catholic bishop of the Seychelles, who recently admitted he watches pornographic movies and has grown marijuana, resigned yesterday after the Vatican called on him to step down. . . ."

—Newspaper wire report, May 1994

was published in England in 1632.

CATHOLIC QUIZ #1
AT THE OSCARS

*There aren't any saints named Oscar, but that hasn't stopped Catholic
actors and makers of Catholic films from coveting the statute (to put
on the nightstand next to the Virgin Mary statue, of course).
How successful were they? Take the quiz and find out.
Answers are on page 195.*

1. It won the hearts of generations of Catholics and the Oscar for
Best Picture in 1965. Even so, its costars (and the citizens of the
town where it was filmed) thought it was a dud. What film was it?

   (A) *Francis of Assisi*

   (B) *The Sound of Music*

   (C) *The Greatest Story Ever Told*

2. What actor was nominated for Best Actor two years in a row
for playing the same Catholic priest in two different films?

   (A) Richard Burton

   (B) Lawrence Olivier

   (C) Bing Crosby

3. Whose performance as a Catholic priest was so spectacular that
he was nominated for Best Actor *and* Best Supporting Actor for
the role?

   (A) Barry Fitzgerald, who played Father Fitzgibbon in *Going My
Way* (1944)

   (B) Eugene Pallette, who played Friar Tuck in *The Adventures
of Robin Hood* (1938)

   (C) Spencer Tracy, who played Father Flanagan in *Boys' Town*
(1938)

Q: How many prostitutes did Pope Alexander VI (1492-1503) take

4. Only one actress has ever won Best Actress for playing a saint. Who was she . . . and what was the movie?

    (A) Ingrid Bergman, who starred in *Joan of Arc* in 1948

    (B) Jennifer Jones, who played Saint Bernadette of Lourdes in *The Song of Bernadette* (1943)

    (C) Siobhan McKenna, who played the Virgin Mary in *King of Kings* (1961)

5. Only one actor has ever won Best Actor for playing a saint. Who was he . . . and what was the movie?

    (A) Graham Faulkner, who played Saint Francis of Assisi in *Brother Son, Sister Moon* (1973)

    (B) Robert Ryan, who played John the Baptist in *King of Kings* (1961)

    (C) Edmund Gwenn, who played Santa Claus (Saint Nicholas) in *Miracle on 34th Street* (1947)

6. What famous Catholic film is believed to have lost the Oscar for Best Picture because its ticket prices were too high?

    (A) *The Song of Bernadette* (1943)

    (B) *The Ten Commandments* (1956)

    (C) *Boys' Town* (1938)

7. Spencer Tracy was ecstatic when he won Best Actor for his portrayal of Father Flanagan in the 1938 film *Boys' Town* . . . but his happiness was shortlived. Why?

    (A) His trophy had been mistakenly inscribed *Dick* Tracy.

    (B) MGM Studios donated his Oscar to the real Boys' Town without his permission.

    (C) Both of the above

    (D) Nun of the above—his car was stolen during the Academy Award ceremony.

to bed with him on an "average" night?   A: 25.

8. What portrayal of a biblical event won the Oscar for Best Special Effects?

   (A) The collapse of the tower of Babel in *The Bible* (1966)

   (B) The parting of the Red Sea in *The Ten Commandments* (1956)

   (C) The miracle of the loaves and fishes in *The Greatest Story Ever Told* (1965)

9. What biblical-period epic won more Oscars than any other film in history?

   (A) *The Ten Commandments* (1956)

   (B) *Ben Hur* (1959)

   (C) *Samson and Delilah* (1949)

10. Barry Fitzgerald won Best Supporting Actor in 1944 for his portrayal of Father Fitzgibbon in *Going My Way*. What made his statue different from every other Oscar statue in history?

   (A) It had a clerical collar.

   (B) It didn't have a head.

   (C) Its arms were folded in prayer . . . and clutched a tiny string of rosary beads.

✠   ✠   ✠

. . . ONE FINAL THOUGHT:

"Everyone knows that damage is done to the soul by bad motion pictures. . . . The more marvelous is the progress of the motion picture art and industry, the more pernicious and deadly has it shown itself to morality, to religion, and even to the very decencies of human society."

                        —Pope Pius XI (1922-1939)

According to Mark 6:2-3, Jesus had four brothers: James, Joses, Juda, and Simon.

CHRISTIAN CRITTERS

You know that doves represent peace in Christian art and lore and that snakes often symbolize the devil —but do you know what other animals represent? Here are some you probably aren't familiar with.

Apes: Sin, malice, sloth, cunning . . . and lust

Donkeys: Humility

Oxen: Jews or Judaism, or humility

Bears: Evil and cruelty

Plain Rats: Evil

White Rats: Day

Black Rats: Night

Gnawing Rats: The ravages of time

Cats: Laziness . . . and lust

Roosters: Watchfulness and vigilance

Dolphins: Resurrection and salvation

Flies: Evil, pestilence

Unicorns: Purity, femininity

White Falcons: Holy men

Wild Falcons: Evil thoughts or actions

Frogs: Plagues, heresy, sin, the devil, materialism

Caterpillars: Life

Cocoons: Death

Butterflies: Resurrection

Grasshoppers or Locusts: The plague

Jesus Holding a Grasshopper: Conversion of whole nations to Christianity

Hogs: Gluttony . . . and lust

Rabbit (Helpless): A Christian

Rabbit (Sexually Aroused): Lust

Rabbit (at the Feet of the Virgin Mary): Her triumph over . . . lust

Horses: The sun . . . and lust

Leopards: Sin, cruelty, the devil, and the antichrist

Owls: Satan

Forty-four percent of U.S. priests and nuns say birth control is "seldom or never" a sin.

HELL ON EARTH

Did you think that all saints are remembered for their great religious works? Think again—some are remembered for the truly miserable lives they led here on earth. Some examples:

SAINT SERAPHINA (1242-1253)

Easily one of the most preposterous and disgusting saint legends the church has to offer. According to one version, Fina was a six-year-old who fell victim to a paralyzing illness and was totally incapacitated for the rest of her life. As if that wasn't bad enough, she asked her parents to lay her out on a hard board instead of in a bed so that she could imitate Jesus' suffering on the cross. They consented—and suffer she did: Seraphina spent the rest of her life on the board and in time developed huge smelly bedsores that attracted rats. (Totally paralyzed, she was unable to fight them off; they attacked her mercilessly.) She festered in this condition for five long years before she died; when her admiring parents finally peeled her off the board, they discovered that it was covered "not with scabs and puss, but with sweet-smelling white violets."

Art Note: Saint Seraphina's most common symbolic attributes are rats and flowers . . . in that order.

SAINT LYDWINA (1380-1433)

Her name literally means "friend of suffering" . . . and for good reason. Lydwina was crippled in an ice-skating accident at the age of sixteen and spent the next thirty-seven years immobile and in great pain, which grew more intense as she got older. For the last nineteen years of her life she couldn't eat anything except communion wafers, and for the last seven she couldn't sleep. She eventually went completely blind . . . and in 1433 she choked to death on her own phlegm. (What does she have to show for all this suffering? No kidding: The church made her the patron saint of ice skaters.)

The U.S. reestablished full diplomatic relations with the Vatican in

SAINT RITA OF CASCIA (1381-1457)

Not long after hearing a sermon on the crown of thorns, Sister Rita felt a sharp piercing pain during her prayers, "as if a thorn had become embedded in her forehead." At first nothing was visible, but over time the spot developed into a huge festering sore; it became so ugly and smelly that her convent forced her to live apart from the other nuns. The wound remained on her forehead for the remaining fifteen years of her life; but when she died in 1457 the wretched stench "became that of roses" overnight. (According to local tradition, her convent in Italy *still* smells of roses.)

Note: Though she rotted in life, Saint Rita apparently stopped rotting after she died—her body is said to have never decomposed and is still on display at her convent in a large coffin-shaped glass case. She is the patron saint of desperate causes and in Italy is more popular than the Virgin Mary.

SAINT BRIGID (c. 450-525)

According to one legendary account of her life, young Brigid was ashamed of her great beauty because it tempted others into sin. So she prayed to God to make her ugly . . . and he delivered: One of her eyes moved to the center of her forehead and grew to enormous size; the other one shriveled away to nothing. It was only then (when marriage understandably seemed hopeless) that her father, a pagan Celtic chieftain, granted her lifelong wish to enter a convent. After she became a nun her eyes miraculously returned to normal, and she went on to found scores of churches, convents, and monasteries. She is the patroness of Ireland.

January 1984, for the first time in 117 years.

THE DEVIL'S DICTIONARY

*Ambrose Bierce, an American newspaper columnist, was the Andy
Rooney of the nineteenth century. Among other things, he wrote a
column called "The Devil's Dictionary." Here are some entries:*

Abstainer, n. A weak person who yields to the temptation of
denying himself a pleasure. A total abstainer is one who abstains
from everything but abstention, and especially from inactivity in
the affairs of others.

Christian, n. One who believes that the New Testament is a
divinely inspired book admirably suited to the spiritual needs of
his neighbor. One who follows the teachings of Christ in so far as
they are not inconsistent with a life of sin.

Convent, n. A place of retirement for women who wish for leisure
to meditate upon the vice of idleness.

Faith, n. Belief without evidence in what is told by one who
speaks without knowledge, of things without parallel.

Feast, n. A festival. A religious celebration usually signalized by
gluttony and drunkenness, frequently in honor of some holy person distinguished for abstemiousness. In the Roman Catholic
Church feasts are "movable" and "immovable," but the celebrants
are uniformly immovable until they are full.

Heaven, n. A place where the wicked cease from troubling you
with talk of their personal affairs, and the good listen with attention while you expound your own.

Infidel, n. In New York, one who does not believe in the Christian religion; in Constantinople, one who does.

Koran, n. A book which the Mohammedans foolishly believe to have been written by divine inspiration, but which Christians know to be a wicked imposture, contradictory to the Holy Scriptures.

Marriage, n. The state or condition of a community consisting of a master, a mistress and two slaves, making in all, two.

Pantheism, n. The doctrine that everything is God, in contradistinction to the doctrine that God is everything.

Piety, n. Reverence for the Supreme Being, based upon His supposed resemblance to man.

Pray, v. To ask that the laws of the universe be annulled in behalf of a single petitioner confessedly unworthy.

Pre-Adamite, n. One of an experimental and apparently unsatisfactory race that antedated Creation and lived under conditions not easily conceived. . . . Little is known of them beyond the fact that they supplied Cain with a wife and theologians with a controversy.

Rack, n. An argumentative implement formerly much used in persuading devotees of a false faith to embrace the living truth.

Redemption, n. Deliverance of sinners from the penalty of their sin, through their murder of the deity against whom they sinned. The doctrine of Redemption is the fundamental mystery of our holy religion, and whoso believeth in it shall not perish, but have everlasting life in which to try and understand it.

Religion, n. A daughter of Hope and Fear, explaining to Ignorance the nature of the Unknowable.

Revelation, n. A famous book in which Saint John the Divine concealed all that he knew. The revealing is done by the commentators, who know nothing.

refused to give up the white robes of his order. Popes have worn white since then.

Reverence, n. The spiritual attitude of a man to a god and a dog to a man.

Rite, n. A religious or semi-religious ceremony fixed by law, precept or custom, with the essential oil of sincerity carefully squeezed out of it.

Saint, n. A dead sinner revised and edited.

Satan, n. One of the Creator's lamentable mistakes, repented in sashcloth and axes. Being instated as an archangel, Satan made himself multifariously objectionable and was finally expelled from Heaven. Halfway in his descent he paused, bent his head in thought a moment and at last went back. "There is one favor that I should like to ask," said he.

"Name it."

"Man, I understand, is about to be created. He will need laws."

"What, wretch! you, his appointed adversary, charged from the dawn of eternity with hatred of his soul—you ask for the right to make his laws?"

"Pardon; what I have to ask is that he be permitted to make them himself."

It was so ordered.

Scriptures, n. The sacred books of our holy religion, as distinguished from the false and profane writings on which all other faiths are based.

Trinity, n. In the multiplex theism of certain Christian churches, three entirely distinct deities consistent with only one. . . . The Trinity is one of the most sublime mysteries of our holy religion. In rejecting it because it is incomprehensible, Unitarians betray their inadequate sense of theological fundamentals. In religion we believe only what we do not understand, except in the instance of an intelligible doctrine that contradicts an incomprehensible one. In that case we believe the former as a part of the latter.

Unction, n. An oiling, or greasing. The rite of extreme unction consists in touching with oil consecrated by a bishop several parts of the body of one engaged in dying. Marbury relates that after the rite had been administered to a certain wicked English nobleman it was discovered that the oil had not been properly consecrated and no other could be obtained. When informed of this the sick man said in anger: "Then I'll be damned if I die!"

"My son," said the priest, "that is what we fear."

RECOMMENDED READING
The Devil's Dictionary, by Ambrose Bierce (New York: Dell Publishing, 1991).

✚　　✚　　✚

SAINT FRANCIS OF ASSISI: A CREATURE OF HABIT
How did Franciscan monks come to wear their trademark Franciscan habits? By chance of fate—at least according to legend: When Saint Francis of Assisi was a young man he sold some of his father's possessions and spent the money restoring an old chapel. His father was so enraged that he brought Francis before the bishop and disinherited him on the spot. To show he didn't have any hard feelings, Francis stripped naked and returned the clothes his father had bought for him. The bishop, shocked by the pious display of nudity, borrowed a rough brown tunic from his gardener and gave it to Francis; he later adopted a similar robe as the habit of his order.

Foot Note: Clerical sandals were another tough habit to break. Today they symbolize religious austerity and sacrifice, but in the old days they didn't—they were just the standard footwear of the Roman Empire. When shoes became popular centuries later, most of the clergy made the switch . . . but some monastic orders didn't.

ordaining his brother a priest and electing him Pope John XIX (1024-31) in one day.

TAKES A FLAYIN', KEEPS ON PRAYIN'

One bizarre but common theme in the legends of the early Christian martyrs is their ability to miraculously survive horrible tortures at the hands of the Roman authorities, who ignore these acts of God and kill them anyway, using some other terrible method. Some examples:

SAINT ADRIAN OF NICOMEDIA (c. 304). Adrian, a Roman soldier, was so impressed by the courage of some Christians he was torturing that he converted to Christianity himself. The Roman authorities ordered him burned to death . . . but a storm smothered the flames.
Final Scene: His executioners pulled him apart over an anvil.

SAINT QUENTIN (c. 287). Quentin, a Roman senator, was thrown in prison after he dropped out of the army and converted to Christianity. Torturers hammered red-hot nails into his forehead and shoulders, but he quickly recovered.
Final Scene: Unimpressed, the torturers impaled Quentin on an iron spit, chopped off his head, tied a millstone around his neck (what was left of it), and threw him into a river.

SAINT PERPETUA AND SAINT FELICITY (203). When they refused to make sacrifices to the pagan gods, Perpetua and Felicity were sentenced to die in the Roman games. They were attacked by wild animals (Perpetua was mauled by a cow), but both survived.
Final Scene: The Roman authorities "sworded them to death."

SAINT AGATHA (date unknown). An attractive girl sworn to holy virginity, Agatha's trouble began when she refused to

Q: What's the only town in the world where Catholics still have to kiss their bishop's

sleep with a Roman consul. He forced her into a brothel, but she managed to stay a virgin even there—which made him so furious that he had her tortured on the rack, beaten with rods, stuck with steel hooks, and burned alive; then he cut off her breasts. The damage was only temporary, though: Saint Peter appeared to her in a vision and healed everything.

Final Scene: The consul rolled her in hot coals containing shards of broken pottery.

SAINT PAUL THE APOSTLE (c. 67). Caught trying to convert some pagans to Christianity, Saint Paul was arrested and thrown to the lions. But he baptized one before it could eat him, and it protected him from the other lions. A few minutes later a hailstorm knocked down one of the arena walls and he escaped.

Final Scene: He was later caught and dragged before the Roman emperor Nero, who ordered him crucified. But Paul protested that as a Roman citizen he had the right to have his head chopped off instead. Nero obliged. After the execution Paul's severed head fell to the ground, bounced three times (in honor of the Trinity), and drenched the executioner with milk spurting from the wounds. Fountains sprang up in the three spots where the head had bounced, each one flowing with miraculous healing waters.

SAINT POLYCARP (c. 155). When a Roman official ordered him to renounce his religion and curse Christ, the elderly Polycarp replied, "I have served him for eighty-six years and he has done me no harm; how can I blaspheme my king and savior?" The official ordered him burned alive, but the flames "made a sort of arch, like a ship's sail filled with the wind . . . round the martyr's body" and would not burn him. So the executioners stabbed him with a sword. That didn't work either: A white dove flew out of the wound along with spurts of blood that smothered the flames.

Final Scene: The guards pulled him out of the fire and speared him to death.

ring when they meet him? A. Hollywood—today's bishops prefer handshakes.

SAINT SEBASTIAN (c. 288). Sebastian, a Roman soldier and closet Christian, was caught red-handed converting other soldiers to Christianity. The Roman emperor Diocletian ordered him shot full of arrows, but he survived.

Final Scene: When Diocletian saw that Sebastian was still alive, he was so shocked that he considered converting to Christianity . . . but then he changed his mind and had Sebastian clubbed to death and thrown into a sewer.

SAINT CATHERINE OF ALEXANDRIA (c. 310). When she refused to renounce Christianity and marry the Roman emperor Maxentius, he ordered that she be ripped to death between two spiked wheels. But lightning struck the wheels and destroyed them as the execution was taking place (the inspiration for Catherine-wheel fireworks), and Catherine's life was spared.

Final Scene: Maxentius had her beheaded.

. . . TAKIN' IT TO EXTREMES

Saint Clement of Ancyra and Saint Agathangelus

"It is the martyr's physical sufferings that lend themselves most readily to amplification," Father Hippolyte Delehaye, a Jesuit scholar and author of *The Legends of the Saints*, wrote in 1905. "The masterpiece of this sort of thing is unquestionably the martyrdom of Saint Clement of Ancyra and Saint Agathangelus. This itinerant martyrdom goes on for no less than twenty-eight years, and is diversified by marvels of very extraordinary kinds.

> . . . To start with, Clement is hung up, his flesh torn with iron combs, and his lips and cheeks battered with stones; he is bound to a wheel, beaten with sticks, and horribly slashed with knives; spikes are thrust into his face, his jaws broken and his teeth pulled out, and his feet are crushed in iron shackles. Then both martyrs are scourged and suspended from a beam; their bodies are scorched with burning torches and they are thrown to wild beasts. Red-hot prongs are forced under their

Top four countries with the most Catholic saints: Italy, Spain, France, and Korea.

nails, and then they are covered with quick-lime and left thus for two days; afterwards strips are torn from their skin and they are whipped again. They are laid on iron grids heated white-hot, and then cast into a fiery furnace where they remain for a day and a night. Once more they are rasped with metal hooks; then a sort of harrow [spiked frame] is set up and they are thrown against its tines. Agathangelus in addition has molten lead poured over his head; he is dragged about the town with a millstone around his neck, and stoned. Clement alone has his ears pierced with red-hot needles, then is burned again with torches, and beaten over the head with a stick. At last, having for several days running received fifty lashes from a whip, he is beheaded, and Agathangelus with him.

Only very rarely have hagiographers [biographers of saints] carried their simplicity of mind, or rather their impudence, to such lengths; the accounts of martyr's sufferings do not ordinarily reach this degree of incredibility.

✛ ✛ ✛

. . . HOLY ROLLERS
The Headlight Christ, Norton, Ohio
Background: On May 1, 1994, a tractor-trailer rig struck a car on Interstate 76 in Norton, Ohio, sending several people to the hospital. The *Akron Beacon Journal* covered the story and ran a picture of the automobile. The next day they were flooded with calls from readers claiming to have seen Jesus in the car headlight in the photograph who wanted to know if the image was a miracle.

What Happened: The paper reexamined the photograph—and lo and behold, there really *was* an image of Jesus in the headlight. They investigated . . . and reported the next day that the owner of the car was deeply religious and had affixed transparent Jesus decals to each headlight. "That's the kind of man he is," his son said later. (No word on whether the decals *caused* the accident.)

Pope John Paul II became auxiliary bishop of Crotch, Poland, in September 1958.

THE UNBELIEVERS

What's the difference between a pagan and a heretic? Between an atheist and an agnostic? You've heard these words before . . . but do you know what they mean? Here's a refresher course.

Heathen: A believer in a religion other than Judaism, Christianity, or Islam.

Pagan: The same thing as a heathen.

Lapsed Catholic: Originally used to describe someone who had left Catholicism and returned to paganism.

Old Catholic: A member of a sect of Catholicism that refuses to believe the pope is infallible.

Spiritist: A person who believes in the ability to communicate with the dead via seances, ouija boards, table tapping, and so forth.

Deist: A person who believes in God, but who believes he (or she or it) did not reveal a particular religion for people to worship.

Pantheist: Someone who believes that all things are part of God.

Agnostic: Someone who believes that there's no proof that God exists but who accepts the possibility that there *might* be a God.

Atheist: A person who is *sure* that God does not exist.

Blasphemer: Someone who speaks irreverently to God or about God.

Heretic: A Catholic who rejects some tenets of the Catholic faith, but not all of them.

Schismatic: Someone who accepts all tenets of the Catholic faith but refuses to acknowledge the authority of the pope.

Apostate: Someone who left the religion they were born into to join another faith.

Infidel: A person who rejects Christianity (for Muslims it means someone who rejects Islam).

Survey result: 58% of priests and 65% of nuns say Catholics who disagree with "some

FALLEN FATHERS

It's not easy being in a priest: In addition to keeping vows of poverty, chastity, and obedience, they have to obey the same laws that the rest of us do. . . . but according to recent newspaper stories, not everyone is up to the task. Here are a few that weren't.

Someone's Falling Lord, Kumbayaaah! In 1983, a student at Colorado State University charged a Fort Collins priest with throwing her down a flight of stairs for playing the tambourine poorly during Mass. According to the student, the priest told her, "You play the same way over and over again. You're not going to play at 5:15 Mass anymore"—and then threw her out the door and down the stairs. (When the Church's youth director tried to stop him, the priest punched her in the face.)

Out of Order. In April 1988, Italian authorities arrested Father Lorenzo Zorza, a New York priest, on charges that he was a money courier for an international heroin and cocaine smuggling ring connected to the Italian Mafia. Zorza was no stranger to the criminal justice system: In 1982 he pled guilty to smuggling stolen Renaissance paintings into the United States; and in 1987 was arrested for trying to sell $40,000 worth of stolen tickets to the Broadway play *Les Miserables* (the charges were later dismissed). Father Zorza, who had been out of contact with his religious order for more than fourteen years, called the drug-related charges "absurd."

Lay Ministry. In July 1990, fifty-six-year-old Archbishop Eugene Marino of Atlanta resigned his archdiocese after only two years at the post, citing personal reasons and a desire to seek "spiritual, medical, and psychological therapy." After a two-month investigation, however, church officials revealed that Marino had been involved in an intimate relationship with a woman for more than

Church teachings" can still be considered "good Catholics."

two years and had been paying the woman $1,500 a month in living expenses. (The archbishop was earning less than $875 a month at the time.) "Love got the best of him," one close friend told reporters. "He played it all on a roll of the dice. He ended up trading the church for her, and now he's lost both of them."

Papal Bull. In July 1991, a French animal-rights group criticized fifty-six-year-old Father Angel Rodriguez, part-time matador and full-time Spanish priest, for using bullfights to raise funds for his parish. Calling Rodriguez an "executioner of unfortunate animals," the group appealed to the Vatican to cancel the annual event, but the Vatican refused. Rodriquez's parishioners supported his unorthodox fundraising practices. "I don't see anything wrong with it," one spectator told reporters. "He's just an ordinary man with his own hobbies."

A Wing and a Prayer. In October 1990, the Nevada Humane Society filed a complaint against the pastor of Saint Peter Canisus Church after he clipped the wings of about one hundred pigeons near his parish. The priest took the action after parishioners complained of being pelted with pigeon droppings. "My intentions were good," he explained. "The clipping of the wings consisted of clipping the long feathers with ordinary house scissors"— a procedure that did not harm the birds. The only problem: The pooping pests became easy prey for local pets, and eighty-three of them were quickly eaten by neighborhood cats and dogs.

Parishable Goods. In February 1992, Father Philip A. Magaldi, a Texas priest, pled guilty to stealing more than $120,000 from his former parish in Providence, Rhode Island. In his guilty plea Magaldi admitted to forging checks, making false statements on church financial reports, and forcing a church volunteer to send him $2,500 worth of the church's weekly collections. Magaldi allegedly spent the money on vacations in Hawaii and the Virgin Islands and on thousands of dollars worth of lottery tickets.

Act of God? According to *The Catholic Almanac*, the Black Death (1347-50)

MYTH-QUOTED?
THE "HISTORICAL JESUS"

*How much of what the gospels say about Jesus of Nazareth
is historically accurate? Not as much as you might think
. . . at least according to one body of scholars.*

PASS IT ON
For many years after Jesus was crucified, the apostles
believed the second coming of Christ was imminent.
Largely because of this, they didn't write his teachings down;
they just spread them by word of mouth. It wasn't until about
70 A.D., scholars speculate, that the early Christians finally
put his life story on paper in the gospel of Mark; the gospel of
John, thought to be the last of the four gospels, wasn't written
until approximately 90 A.D.

By then the story of Jesus' life had been embellished by
generations of storytelling—and in the centuries that followed, the words, parables, and miracles attributed to him
would be told, recorded, translated into new languages,
retold, and reinterpreted more often than probably any other
collection of teachings in the history of mankind. (As if that
isn't enough, mainstream biblical scholars now believe that
none of the four gospel authors knew Jesus firsthand.)

THE BIG QUESTION
Was something lost in the shuffle? Yes, many experts say.
While some parts of the Gospels describe actual events in the life
of Jesus, many other parts, they believe, are based on folklore or
legend, and were added by the early Christians after his death in
order to clarify and interpret his teachings for future generations.
The only problem: Nobody knows for sure anymore which of the
tales are factual and which ones are legendary. Over the centuries,

wiped out 25-30% of the population of Europe . . . and 40% of the clergy.

the scholars argue, the distinction between what Jesus' followers *say* he did and what he *really* did has been lost.

THE JESUS SEMINAR
That's what the folks at the Jesus Seminar are trying to figure out. Founded in 1985, the seminar is a group of more than two hundred Catholic, Protestant, and non-Christian scholars from universities and theological institutions around the world. Drawing from fields as diverse as archaeology, anthropology, sociology, and literary analysis, they met twice a year through 1991 to study and debate the authenticity of nearly 500 sayings—33 parables, 290 aphorisms, 81 dialogues, and 90 stories—that the New Testament and other sources attribute to Jesus.

The seminar is controversial to say the least: Jacob Neusner, a professor of religious studies at the University of South Florida, calls it "either the greatest scholarly hoax since the Piltdown man or the utter bankruptcy of New Testament studies—I hope the former." Not everyone agrees with that analysis, however. "These are not maverick scholars," says Father Edward F. Beutner, a participating Catholic priest. "They take a very careful approach to how sayings of Jesus were transmitted and to the evolution of the Bible texts."

THE AYES HAVE IT
Despite the controversy, sifting through biblical texts to find the authentic words of Jesus is nothing new—people as diverse as Albert Schweitzer and Thomas Jefferson have been doing it since the late eighteenth century, when some biblical scholars first abandoned the notion that the Bible is historically accurate.

But the Jesus Seminar takes a novel approach: It actually *votes* on whether specific passages are authentic. Scholars drop colored beads into a box—red for yes, pink for maybe, gray for probably, and black for no—then they tally the results and release them to the public. The method is simplistic but effective, says Bernard Scott, one participant. "It enables ordinary people to see in a sim-

Q: What was Saint Francis of Assisi's first name?   A. John. He was

ple way a consensus by group of scholars. It alerts people that everything in the Bible is not the same from a historical viewpoint."

FINDINGS

The scholars admit their efforts aren't perfect. "This is not a final take on what Jesus said," Hal Taussig, the seminar's spokesman, concedes. Rather, it is more of a best-guess attempt to understand the "historical Jesus"—Jesus as he really lived, as opposed to the Jesus of traditional religious belief. Some of their conclusions:

• **Jesus said only about 20 percent of the things attributed to him.**
All told, 31 sayings in the 4 gospels and several apocryphal sources won enough red votes to be considered authentic; another two hundred quotes fell into the pink category—creating a combined total of about 20 percent. Another 30 percent of the attributed quotes fell into the gray category ("A gray vote meant that some of the *ideas* may have gone back to Jesus, but not the *words*," Funk says); and the remaining 50 percent received black votes, the equivalent of a vote of no confidence.

• **He didn't say** *anything* **the gospel of John says he did.** "Most scholars, if they had worked through the sayings as we had," says Robert Fortna, one of the participants "would tend to agree there is virtually nothing in the fourth Gospel [John] that goes back to Jesus." Statements like "I am the good shepherd," "I am the bread of life," and "I am the light of the world" are mostly the work of the author, not Jesus, the seminar argues.

• **He never said the Lord's Prayer . . . but he did say some of the things in it.** According to the gospels of Matthew and Luke, Jesus taught the Lord's Prayer (the Our Father) to his disciples. . . . but the seminar has concluded that he probably didn't. Specifically, he didn't ask God to "deliver us from evil," and most likely never said, "thy kingdom come; thy will be done." The scholars do believe that he said *some* of the things in the prayer and that other

called Francis because his father (some people say his mother) was French.

parts of it "represent his ideas." He just never taught all of the concepts together in the form of a single prayer.

• **He only said three of the eight beatitudes attributed to him in the gospels of Matthew (5:3-12) and Luke (6:20-23).** Jesus said, "Blessed are the poor in spirit, for theirs is the kingdom of heaven"; "Blessed are the hungry, for they shall be filled"; and "Blessed are those who mourn, for they shall be comforted"—but he didn't say "Blessed are the meek, for they shall inherit the earth"; "Blessed are the peacemakers, for they shall be called sons of God"—or any of the other beatitudes. And, the scholars speculate, the author of Luke inserted four of his own "woes" into his Gospel (woe to the rich, the satiated, and so forth) to counterbalance his four "blesseds." Luke had "a strong kind of sympathy for the poor over the rich," one scholar speculates.

• **He didn't predict that the world would end . . . or that he, as the Son of Man, would sit in judgment.** According to most mainstream biblical scholars—even those not participating in the seminar—Jesus often spoke of the kingdom of God . . . but seldom talked about himself. After his death, the scholars believe, the early church "invented sayings in which Jesus described his identity in terms that included a future role as the 'Son of Man.'"

• **He didn't ask God, "Why hast thou forsaken me?" during the crucifixion.** "My God, my God, why hast thou forsaken me?" is also the first sentence of Psalm 22 of the Old Testament. Scholars believe that the author of the gospels of Matthew and Mark put the words into Jesus' mouth to demonstrate that he was fulfilling the Old Testament prophesy of the coming of the Messiah.

. . . But he really did say most of the parables attributed to him—including those about the Good Samaritan and the Prodigal Son. "The parables that got the most recommendations had several things in common," Bernard Scott says. "They are all parables that are derived from everyday life. . . . The 'Good Samaritan' got the most votes." The ones believed to be written by others, he

says, "reflected the church trying to understand itself. . . . They just weren't good stories."

OTHER FINDINGS
• Jesus didn't call on his followers to preach the Gospel to all nations—or anyone other than Jews, for that matter. He "did not anticipate a mission to the Gentiles," says Funk, the seminar's founder.

• He really did tell people to "turn the other cheek" and to give money without promise of its return.

• The conversations Jesus had with his disciples at the Last Supper weren't the ones that are recorded in the Bible. This is significant, since a large portion of the Catholic Mass is taken from the gospel version of the Last Supper.

RECOMMENDED READING
The Five Gospels: The Search for the Authentic Words of Jesus, by Robert W. Funk, Roy W. Hoover, and the Jesus Seminar (Macmillan, 1993).

✚ ✚ ✚

. . . A SAINT FOR REGULAR FOLKS
Saint Homobonus (d. 1197). The patron saint of tailors and clothworkers, Homobonus was a happily married cloth worker who spent most of his free time at church and gave a lot of money to charity. That's about it—had he not jumped up one day during Mass, stretched his arms out in the shape of a cross, and dropped dead on the floor (no one realized he was dead until *after* Mass had ended), he would have been a completely and utterly unremarkable fellow. . . . So why did Pope Innocent III canonize him two years later? As the Pope put it, "he did ordinary things very well."

Pope Hormisdas (514-23) had a son; *he* was elected Pope Silverius in 536.

MARITAL AID

*One of the big drawbacks of a celibate clergy is that the Church's
advice on sexual matters gets pretty strange at times.
Some examples:*

"Young woman, if you are going to be married to that young man, I
will tell you what to do. First, try as much as you can not to be
alone with him, especially at night, or in the dark, or in secret, or
in lonesome places. Try not to have long conversations with him,
or have long walks with him."

—**Saint Alphonsus Liguori (1696-1787)**

"When, for the first time, [a young woman] participates in the
greatest physical expression of the love of one human for another,
she will want Almighty God, also, to take part in that fulfillment
by bestowing His blessing upon it. . . . She will want to give herself
to her husband as the most perfect gift that she can bestow upon
someone whom she will love very much. Will she, then, want to
give him a second-hand wedding present?"

—*A Catholic Parent's Guide to Sex Education,* **1962**

"While 'frigidity' exists in some marriages, one suspects that it is
less prevalent than popular writers would have us imagine. . . . A
wife should not expect to achieve an orgasm in each act; for her,
there probably will be no definite and complete ending to intercourse at times. Nor should she achieve an orgasm for her physical
or emotional satisfaction. If she seeks to fulfill the needs of her husband rather than herself, she will often feel a deep sense of accom-
plishment in her very communion with him."

—*Marriage Guide for Engaged Catholics,* **1961**

"Marriage is not good, but it is good in comparison with fornication."

—**Saint Augustine (354-430)**

"One problem that may arise on some occasions is that of 'trial marriage.' A young engaged couple mean, by this, the commencement of sexual relations before marriage, their argument for it being that . . . they wish to make certain that they are 'physically compatible' before they take the final step. This is, of course, nothing more or less than an attempt to excuse their lack of control to their own consciences. . . . From the medical viewpoint there is no such thing as physical incompatibility except in cases of anatomical defect, which can, in every case, be detected if the couple visit their doctor for a premarital medical examination."
—*A Catholic Parent's Guide to Sex Education*

"Matrimony is always a vice; all that can be done is to excuse it; therefore it was made a religious sacrament."
—St. Jerome (342-420)

"[Birth control] should always be the exceptional situation in marriage, never the normal. Even when family limitation is permissible, the methods you use may well make the whole process evil. This is what some people find hard to understand. Having a good reason does not make everything you do right, else many more drunken husbands or nagging wives might be in their graves. The end does not necessarily justify the means. A soldier might get soft living in Korea by selling out his country, or might win a battle for his country by wantonly slaughtering hundreds of women and children to get at a machine-gun nest. Neither course of conduct would receive the approval of American public opinion."
—*The Catholic Marriage Manual*, 1958

"May it be hoped that we shall soon have progressed from this era, where it is not unknown for a mother, asked how babies originate, to reply: 'You'll know soon enough, my girl, when you've been caught!' "
—*A Catholic Parent's Guide to Sex Education*

Clare of Assisi the patron saint of television. (Why her? She used to have visions.)

"A good Christian is due in one and the same woman to love the creature of God . . . but to hate in her the corrupting and mortal conjugal connection, sexual intercourse, and all that pertains to her as a wife."

—Saint Augustine (354-430)

✛ ✛ ✛

ELVIS PRESLEY, BIBLE PREACHER

Okay, okay . . . Elvis wasn't Catholic—and according to more than one source he was an anti-Catholic bigot—but the King had a lot of interesting things to say about the Bible . . . at least according to the authors of Elvis: What Happened?

"There were times," says Sonny, "when Presley, half-way through a Bible reading, would stop and interpret, and change the wording. There is a passage somewhere in the Bible which mentions that a rich man, if he is only rich, cannot get into heaven. Well, Elvis turned that around and would tell us, 'The Bible says that a rich man's chance of getting into heaven is like a camel's ass trying to get through the eye of the needle.' Now that wasn't meant to be funny. We weren't supposed to laugh at that. Then he would say, 'Well the Bible didn't mean it that way, because I'm rich and I'm going to heaven.' We would always nod our heads and agree."

. . . Sonny recalls that the Bible teachings were really a scream, but nobody dared laugh. Presley was deadly serious. Sonny recalls: ". . . He would say the funniest things in quoting the Bible. Now whenever he mentioned Jesus, he would just say aside, 'Now, Jesus, he was getting it on with Mary, the woman at the well, you know, Mary Magdeline. It ain't in the Bible but it's true. She got stoned, but Jesus took care of her and they traveled around a lot together.' " . . . Red West recalls, "He would say, 'Jesus said he was old and of age and he fell ass backwards in the dust.' Later on, after we got together, we would laugh our heads off because it was hysterical."

RECOMMENDED READING

Elvis: What Happened? (Ballantine Books, 1977), the funniest book on Elvis ever written—and still available in paperback.

Sixty percent of U.S. nuns say their lives are "better than they anticipated."

HOLIDAY HAPPENINGS

You know that Santa Claus comes on Christmas Day and that the Easter Bunny comes at Easter . . . but what about other religious holidays? Here are some traditions that aren't as well known.

Saint Agnes Eve (January 20). Young girls who fast for twenty-four hours and then eat a salted egg just at bedtime will meet their future husbands in their dreams that night. (That's all that's supposed to happen—Agnes is the patron saint of virgins.)

Saint Paul's Day (January 25). Today's weather predicts the future for the coming year: A sunny day means a good year; rain or snow means an "indifferent" year; mist means crop failures and food shortages; and thunder or wind means that "many people are doomed to die."

Candlemas (February 2). Traditionally the day the candles used at Mass during the year are consecrated; also the day when German farmers predict the weather by watching badgers as they come out of hibernation: If the badger sees his shadow, it means there will be six more weeks of winter. If he doesn't, spring will begin early—and the farmers can begin to plant their crops. (Sound familiar? It should: When German immigrants settled in Pennsylvania in the nineteenth century, there weren't any badgers there for them to watch . . . so they kept an eye on *groundhogs* instead. February 2 is also Groundhog Day.)

Saint Valentine's Day (February 14). "Let a single woman go out of her own door very early in the morning, and if the first person she meets be a woman, she will not be married that year; if she meets a man she will be married within three months." (Also the day that birds choose their mates and "couple fervently in the woods.")

Saint Mark's Day (April 25). If you put a watch on the front porch of your church and keep it there from 11:00 P.M. to 1:00 A.M., you can see the ghosts of your loved ones who are going to die in the coming year walk into the church. Too depressing? If you're an unmarried woman, try this one instead: Leave a flower on the porch and return at midnight . . . and you'll see a ghostly apparition of your future husband. (No word on what you'll see if he's one of the people slated to die.)

Saint Medard's Day (June 8). Medard is known as "the great pisser" to French Catholics, who believed that if it rained on his saint day, it would rain for the next forty days as well. (According to historian Will Durant, "If it failed to pour, his impatient worshippers, now and then, threw his statue into the water.")

Saint Swithin's Eve (July 14). "Select three things you most wish to know; write them down with a new pen and red ink on a sheet of fine wove paper, from which you must previously cut off all the corners and burn them. Fold the paper into a true lover's knot, and wrap round it three hairs from your head. Place the paper under your pillow for three successive nights, and your curiosity to know the future will be satisfied."

Saint Swithin's Day (July 15). Another weather-predicting day. Reason: Saint Swithin wanted to be buried in a church cemetery so that "the sweet rain of heaven might fall upon his grave," but his fellow monks interred him in a cathedral instead. It rained continuously for the next forty days and nights—until the brothers reburied him in the churchyard. The rain stopped . . . and a new tradition started: If it rains on St. Swithin's Day, it will rain for the next forty; if it's sunny, the opposite is true.

Saint Anne's Day (July 26). Named in honor of the Virgin Mary's mom. On this day, unmarried women searched for a pea pod containing nine peas and put it on the floor near their front door with a note that read, "Come on in, my dear, and do not fear." The first guy to come in through the door is the woman's future husband.

Saint Michael's Day/Michaelmas (September 29). "If you eat goose on Michaelmas, you never want money all year round."

Saint Andrew's Day (November 30). For some reason, on this day ghosts return to their buried treasure to see if it's still undisturbed. Result: According to author John Steinbeck, on this day "all buried treasure sends up a faint phosphorescent glow through the ground"—which defeats the purpose of checking it in the first place, since glow-in-the-dark treasure is pretty easy to find.

✛ ✛ ✛

. . . A SICK YOLK

"A panic terror of the end of the world seized the good people of Leeds, England, and its neighborhood in the year 1806. It arose from the following circumstances. A hen, in a village close by, laid eggs, on which were inscribed the words, 'Christ is coming.' Great numbers visited the spot, and examined these wondrous eggs, convinced that the day of judgment was near at hand. Like sailors in a storm, expecting every instant to go to the bottom, the believers suddenly became religious, prayed violently, and flattered themselves that they repented them of their evil courses. But a plain tale soon put them down, and quenched their religion entirely. Some gentlemen, hearing of the matter, went one fine morning, and caught the poor hen in the act of laying one of her miraculous eggs. They soon ascertained beyond doubt that the egg had been inscribed with some corrosive ink, and cruelly forced up again into the bird's body. At this explanation, those who had prayed, now laughed, and the world wagged as merrily as of yore."

—**Charles Mackay,** *Extraordinary Popular Delusions and the Madness of Crowds,* 1841

Pope Pius XII (1939-1958) was the first pontiff to own a rowing machine.

LATIN LINGO

*Latin is the traditional language of the Catholic Church . . .
so it stands to reason that a lot of religious words
we use come from Latin. Some examples:*

Pagan: From *paganus*, the Latin word for "peasant," a tiller of the soil. (Peasants, who lived out in the country-side, were among the last classes of people to convert to Christianity.)

Mass: The name is believed to come from phrase that ended the Latin Mass: *Ite, missa est*, which means, "Go, you are dismissed."

Profanity: From *pro* and *fanum*, which mean "outside the temple," or "unholy."

Fanatic: Also from the Latin word *fanum*; originally meant "inspired by God."

Infidel: From *infidelis*, which means "having no faith."

Sacred: From *sacer*, the Latin word for "set apart." ("Sacrifice" has the same root.)

Crucify: From *crux* and *figo*, the Latin words for "cross" and "affix."

Cardinal: Possibly from *cardo*, which meant hinge (the cardinals were the "hinge" on which many church operations turned).

Cloister: From *claustrum*, which means "enclosed space." ("Claustrophobia" has the same root.)

Pastor: From *pasco*, the Latin word meaning "feed." ("Pasture" has the same root.)

Genuflect: From the Latin words *genu*, meaning "knee," and *flectere*, "to bend."

Morals: From *mores*, the Latin word for "customs."

Nun: From *nonna*, the word for "child's nurse."

Rosary: From *rosarium*, which means "rose garden."

Pulpit: From *pulpitum*, the Latin word for "platform."

Friar: From *frater*, the Latin word for "brother."

The Apostles never said the Apostles' Creed. The prayer

MAKE NO MISTAKES

Ever wonder how the pope became infallible?
It's not a pretty story.

THE CONTROVERSY

Today the Church teaches that the pope is infallible "in matters of faith and morals" . . . but that hasn't always been the case—papal infallibility didn't become an official part of church teachings until July 18, 1870, when the First Vatican Council made it a part of church dogma for the first time. Before 1870 the idea was controversial even among *popes*, who supposedly stood to gain the most from it. Reason: Papal infallibility was originally conceived as a means of *limiting* the power of individual popes by preventing them from undoing the work of their predecessors.

The idea was the brainchild of Peter Olivi, an "eccentric Franciscan, repeatedly accused of heresy," who cooked it up in 1280 to prevent future popes from rescinding a ruling that Pope Nicholas III (1277-1280) had made favoring the Franciscan order. Nicholas went along with papal infallibility, but subsequent pontiffs didn't: Pope John XXII (1316-1334) denounced it as "a work of the devil . . . the Father of Lies" and in 1324 issued a papal bull condemning it as heresy. Thanks to his opposition and that of like-minded popes, cardinals, and bishops over the centuries, the idea remained a pipe dream for the next 546 years . . . and probably still would be today were it not for the efforts of one man: Pope Pius IX (1846-1878), the longest-reigning pope in history and a man historians describe as the father of the modern papacy.

A POPE AND HIS COUNCIL

Pius IX was elected pope on June 16, 1846, at a time when popes were absolute rulers of the Papal States, a Church-controlled region of central Italy that was the precursor to the modern-day Vatican City. Pius succeeded Pope Gregory XVI (1831-1846), an

wasn't formalized until the 8th century A.D.

archconservative, repressive pontiff who was so unpopular that he depended on Austrian and papal troops to crush the antipapal rebellions that regularly threatened his reign. Pius, on the other hand, had a reputation as a liberal reformer and was an extremely popular pope . . . at least at first: In his first two years as pope he declared an amnesty for political prisoners, relaxed press censorship, and granted a constitution that shared governmental power with an elected parliament of laypeople. But in April 1848 he refused to approve the parliament's declaration of war to expel Austria from northern Italy (Austria's Emperor Ferdinand was Catholic); and this, combined with the economic collapse of the Papal States, caused his popularity to disappear overnight. Rome exploded into open revolt: On November 15 the pope's prime minister was stabbed to death by an assassin, and nine days later an angry mob surrounded the papal palace, forcing Pius to flee for his life disguised as a simple priest.

Back in Business
French troops crushed the rebellion a few months later, and Pius returned to Rome in April 1850. But he was a changed man—his liberal sympathies having given way to antirevolutionary paranoia, shortly after returning to Rome he scrapped his reforms and devoted the rest of his papacy to waging war against liberalism and centralizing Church authority within the hands of the papacy. His crowning achievement came in 1869-1870, when he convened the First Vatican Council and used it to proclaim papal infallibility as an official part of Church dogma.

VATICAN I: THE OFFICIAL STORY
The general council opened its doors on December 8, 1869, and remained in session until July 18, 1870. Work on the papal infallibility dogma began in the middle of May and lasted until July 18, when a bishop read the final language of the statement before the assembled prelates and submitted it to a vote:

> We teach and define as a divinely revealed dogma, that when the Roman pontiff speaks *ex cathedra*—that is, when

Q. What were the names of the Virgin Mary's parents?

he, using his office as pastor and teacher of all Christians, in virtue of his apostolic office, defines a doctrine on faith and morals to be held by the whole Church—he, by the divine assistance promised to him in the blessed Peter, possesses that infallibility with which the Divine Redeemer was pleased to invest his Church in the definition of doctrine on faith and morals, and that therefore, such definitions of the Roman Pontiff are irreformable in their own nature and not because of the consent of the Church.

Of the 598 bishops still in Rome, 533 voted yes, 2 voted no, and 63 abstained from voting to avoid a public show of disagreement with the pope. Immediately after the final tally was announced, the two no votes (Bishop Riccio of Cajazzo, Sicily, and Bishop Fitzgerald of Little Rock, Arkansas) dropped to their knees in front of the pope and in a show of unanimity proclaimed, "Now I believe" (to which Pius supposedly responded, "Good fellow!"). In the following months the sixty-three dissenting prelates consented as well; and for the first time in history, the pope was officially considered infallible in matters of faith and morals.

WHAT REALLY HAPPENED

How did Pius manage to pull off a task that had eluded other popes for more than nineteen hundred years? Catholic theologian Hans Küng identifies four major reasons: "Pius IX had a sense of divine mission which he carried to extremes; he engaged in double-dealing; he was mentally disturbed; and he misused his office.

> . . . So repressive were the agenda and official procedures; so one-sided and partisan were the selection of main theological experts and the composition of both the conciliar commissions and the conciliar presidium; so numerous were the means of pressure (moral, psychological, church-political, newspaper campaigns, threatened withdrawal of financial support, harassment by the police) to which the bishops of the anti-Infallibilist minority *and* the Infallibilist majority were exposed; so varied were the forms of manipulation applied, at the pope's behest, to advance the definition

A. Joachim and Anne.

before, during, and after the Council that . . . as painful and embarrassing as it may be to admit, this Council resembled a well-organized and manipulated totalitarian party congress rather than a free gathering of Christian people.

Küng argues that Pope Pius IX compromised the council's freedom so severely that the infallibility doctrine it promulgated cannot be considered a valid teaching of the Church. (Largely because of his unorthodox views on papal infallibility, in 1979 Küng was forbidden by the Vatican from teaching theology in the name of the Catholic Church.)

PAPAL BULLY

Küng isn't alone in his condemnation of Vatican I and papal infallibility: In 1979 Father August Bernhard Hasler, a Catholic priest, historian, and former staff member of the Vatican's Secretariat for Christian Unity, published *How the Pope Became Infallible: Pius IX and the Politics of Persuasion,* a two-volume account of the First Vatican Council. Using documents in the Vatican archives that to this day have never been released to scholars or the general public, Father Hasler painted a picture of the proceedings—and of Pope Pius himself—that differs greatly from the Vatican's version of the truth:

• **Pius may have been nuts.** He suffered from severe seizures for nearly his entire life (it was the only reason he entered the priesthood instead of joining the Pope's Noble Guard, his first career choice)—and as a young priest the future pontiff once admitted in a letter to Pope Leo XII that he suffered from memory loss and could not think clearly for extended periods of time. By 1869 the ravages of his disease, combined with the stress of his office and his advancing age (he was seventy-eight when Vatican I opened its doors), took their toll on his psychological state, making him unpredictable, irrational, emotional, dictatorial . . . as well as a virtual megalomaniac. At times he even suffered from delusions of grandeur, as historian Ferdinand Gregorovius observed one after-

Q. How many beads are there in a standard rosary?

noon in 1870: "The pope recently got the urge to try out his infallibility. . . . While out on a walk he called to a paralytic: 'Get up and walk.' The poor devil gave it a try and collapsed, which put [the pope] very much out of sorts. The anecdote has already been mentioned in the newspapers. I really believe that he's insane."

RIGGING THE COUNCIL

. . . As if that wasn't bad enough, Pius was also dishonest. "In my entire life," Cardinal Gustav von Hohenlohe told a friend, "I have never met a man who was less particular about the truth than Pius IX." Other bishops, including Bishop Henri Maret, a French theologian, openly referred to the Pope as a liar . . . and it is thanks in large part to Pius's dogged determination and his dishonesty, Hasler and others argue, that Pius was able to pull off Vatican I in the first place. Take a look, for example, at how he behaved during the council:

• **He stacked the council's planning committees with his own supporters.** Of the ninety-six consulting positions, fifty-nine went to Italians (the pope's strongest supporters); thirty-seven went to church officials from other countries. And of these thirty-seven, only six had any experience working in the Vatican. In time some of the inexperienced came to believe they had been appointed to the committee for the sole purpose of being outmaneuvered by the pope's supporters. One of them, Bishop Joseph Karl Hefele of Rottenberg, complained to a friend, "The longer I stay here, the more clearly I see the duplicity behind my appointment as a *consultor concilii*. That was just Rome's way of hoodwinking the public with the appearance of neutrality. In reality I have no idea what I'm supposed to be doing here."

• **He insisted that the council be convened in Saint Peter's Basilica, which had notoriously bad acoustics.** It was almost impossible for the bishops—particularly the elderly ones—to hear what was going on; many began to suspect that Pius had chosen the basilica purposely for this reason. "I now sit right next to the

A. Fifty-nine.

Secretary's desk," Bishop Hefele of Tübengen wrote, "in the immediate vicinity of the cardinals . . . but often I can't hear what's being said from the speaker's platform."

The pope made the situation worse by refusing to allow copies of the speeches to be printed (which prevented the bishops from studying them carefully); by banning small group discussions of the speeches (the ban was later extended to large groups as well); and by only allowing committee members (all of whom supported infallibility) the right to reply to a speech immediately after it had been given. Everyone else had to make an appointment a day in advance, *before* they knew what the speech was going to be about. Pius put all of these restrictions into effect *without* consulting the bishops; in previous ecumenical councils the bishops themselves had set the rules for debate.

• **He drove the bishops until they literally dropped from illness and exhaustion.** Pius refused to postpone the council or call a recess under any circumstances, even when the summer heat and a malaria epidemic caused scores of bishops to become seriously ill. When Pius learned of their condition, he reportedly shouted, "*Che crepino pure*"—"Let them croak." Such remarks apparently were not unusual: When John Acton, an English historian, heard the remark he exclaimed, "What wild passion!" "That isn't just passion," a Roman bishop replied. "That's his personality."

Pius also bullied dissenting bishops into supporting him. One example: When Archbishop Bathiarian of Armenia refused to support infallibility, the papal police tried to arrest his personal secretary, sparking a small riot in the process. The incident so spooked the other Armenian bishops they demanded permission to return home immediately. (The Pope refused . . . but two of them fled anyway.)

• **He used financial pressure against the bishops.** More than 350 of the bishops were totally financially dependent on the Vatican, a fact that Pius took advantage of by threatening to cut off dissenters without a cent. He enforced the threat by requiring that all

Q. What is the name of the yearly offering collected by parishes and given to the pope?

voting be conducted in public. The tactic worked: All of the financially dependent bishops voted in favor of the pope—as one bishop put it, "My bread is in one camp, my convictions in another."

THE OUTCOME
Many of the bishops assembled in Rome were so disgusted with the proceedings that they simply stopped attending. "I'm not going to the Council anymore," Bishop Felix Dupanloup wrote in his diary in June of 1870. "The violence, the shamelessness, and even more the falsity, vanity, and continual lying force me to keep my distance." Bishop François Lecourtier of France was another dissenter. He complained that

> An imposing minority, representing the faith of more than one hundred million Catholics, that is, almost half the entire Church, is crushed beneath the yoke of a restrictive agenda, which contradicts conciliar traditions. It is crushed by commissions which have not been truly elected and which dare to insert undebated paragraphs in the texts after debate has closed. It is crushed by the absolute absence of discussion, response, objections, and the opportunity to demand explanations; by newspapers which have been encouraged to hunt the bishops down and to incite the clergy against them.

(Lecourtier was so discouraged by the proceedings that he threw his conciliar documents in the Tiber River and left Rome before the final vote was taken. After the council had ended, Pius retaliated by firing him from his bishopric.)

According to one estimate, at the opening of the council Pius IX could count on the support of only about 50 bishops: Another 130 were opposed, and the rest were undecided. But thanks to his powers of persuasion (and coercion . . . and retribution), on July 18 Pius IX got his way; and to this day the church teaches that the pope is infallible in matters of faith and morals.

A. Peter's Pence.

THE AFTERMATH

. . . As for Pius himself, however, his satisfaction was short lived: The day after the vote on infallibility was held, the Franco-Prussian war broke out and the French government withdrew the troops that had been protecting Rome from the territorial ambitions of the Kingdom of Sardinia (it had annexed all of the Papal States except Rome in September 1860). As soon as the French military left town the Italian troops moved in . . . and on September 20, 1870, annexed all of Rome except Vatican City itself. Pius suspended the Vatican Council on October 20 and never reconvened it; he lived out the rest of his days as a self-styled "prisoner of the Vatican," the first infallible pope . . . and the first one in centuries without a kingdom.

RECOMMENDED READING

How the Pope Became Infallible, by August Bernard Hasler (Doubleday, 1981), *a great book—probably the best one on the subject.*

Infallible?—An Inquiry, by Hans Küng (Doubleday, 1970), *the book that caused the Vatican to ban Küng from teaching theology in the name of the church.*

The Church in Crisis: A History of the General Councils, 325-1870, by Philip Hughes (Doubleday, 1961).

✤ ✤ ✤

. . . CARMELITE KNOWLEDGE.

"A woman listed in court papers as Jane Doe filed suit against a California priest today claiming he coerced her into having sex with him in 1985 while she was studying to be a nun. According to court documents, the priest told the ex-nun that her religious vows *required* her to have sex with him so that he could get over his 'fixation with the female body' and become a better priest."
— **Newspaper Wire Report, June 1992**

SUFFER THE LITTLE CHILDREN

*Here's a look at some of the writings of the Reverend J. Furniss,
C.S.S.R. He's probably the most severely disurbed children's
author the Catholic Church has ever produced.*

STORYTIME
When you think of children's literature, do you think of
The Cat in the Hat? Dick and Jane? Nancy Drew and the
Hardy Boys? . . . Then you haven't read *Tracts for Spiritual Reading,* a children's book that Father Furniss, an Irish priest, wrote for
the children of Ireland in the 1800s. His book met with church
approval; in his introduction to the book, the vicar general of
Dublin wrote, "I have carefully read over this Little Volume for
Children and have found nothing whatever in it contrary to the
doctrines of Holy Faith; but on the contrary, a great deal to
charm, instruct, and edify the youthful classes for whose benefit it
has been written." See if you agree . . .

HELL: THE GUIDED TOUR
"Come into this room. You see it is very small. But see, in the
midst of it there is a girl, perhaps about eighteen years old. What a
terrible dress she has on—her dress is made of fire. On her head
she wears a bonnet of fire. It is pressed down close all over her
head; it burns her head, it burns into the skin; it scorches the bone
of the skull and makes it smoke. The red hot fiery heat goes into
the brain and melts it . . . there she will stand for ever burning and
scorched! She counts with her fingers the moments as they pass
away slowly, for each moment seems to her like a hundred years.
As she counts the moments she remembers that she will have to
count them for ever and ever. . . .

(62,824 of them were granted to couples in the United States).

"LOOK INTO THIS LITTLE PRISON. In the middle of it there is a boy, a young man. He is silent, despair is on him. . . . His eyes are burning like two burning coals. Two long flames come out of his ears. His breathing is difficult. Sometimes he opens his mouth and breath of blazing fire rolls out of it. But listen! There is a sound just like that of a kettle boiling. Is it really a kettle which is boiling? No; then what is it? Hear what it is. The blood is boiling in the scalding veins of that boy. The brain is boiling and bubbling in his head. The marrow is boiling in his bones. Ask him why he is thus tormented. His answer is that when he was alive, his blood boiled to do very wicked things. . . .

"YOU ARE GOING TO SEE AGAIN THE CHILD about which you read in the Terrible Judgment, that it was condemned to hell. See! it is a pitiful sight. The little child is in this red hot oven. Hear the fire! It beats its head against the roof of the oven. It stamps its little feet on the floor. You can see on the face of this little child what you see on the faces of all in hell—despair, desperate and horrible. . . . This child committed very bad mortal sins, knowing well the harm of what it was doing, and knowing that hell would be the punishment. God was very good to this child. Very likely God saw that this child would get worse and worse, and would never repent, and so it would have to be punished much more in hell. So God, in His mercy, called it out of the world in its early childhood. . . .

"THERE ARE SOME DISEASES SO BAD, such as cancers and ulcers, that people cannot bear to breathe the air in the house where they are. There is something worse. It is the smell of death coming from a dead body lying in the grave. The dead body of Lazarus had been in the grave only four days. Yet Martha, his sister, could not bear that it should be taken out again. But what is the smell of death in hell? St. Bonaventure says that if one single body was taken out of hell and laid on the earth, in that same moment every living creature on the earth would sicken and die. Such is the smell of death from one body in hell.

Q: What is the pope's white skullcap called? (Hint: It isn't called a yarmulke.)

WHY THE POINTY HAT?

It's probably not the biggest question facing the Catholic Church today . . . but it still deserves to be asked: Why does the clergy dress so funny? The answer is surprisingly secular.

CLOTHES CALL

A Clothing was probably the last thing the apostles and early Christians had on their minds in the years following the crucifixion: Because they believed the second coming of Christ was imminent, they didn't bother to formalize many aspects of their new religion. Clerical dress was no exception—nobody gave any thought to what priests should wear during Mass; they just wore the same clothes that laypeople did. As author Adrian Fortescue put it in his book *The Vestments of the Roman Rite*, "Every vestment now worn by a Latin priest, every one worn by a Latin bishop (except the mitre), represents an article of ordinary Roman dress, such as was worn by Christians all over the Roman Empire in the second, third and fourth centuries."

Fashions changed over time, but the priests didn't: They stuck with the same clothes they had always worn . . . until their garments became so different from what everyone else was wearing that they were associated exclusively with religious life. Some examples:

THE MITRE

Description: The pointed hat that popes and bishops wear (like the one at the top of the page). The *Catholic Encyclopedia* describes it as "a folding hat, made up of two equal, cone-shaped parts that rise to a divided peak at the top." It gets its name from *mitra*, the Greek word for "turban."

Origin: Why does the pope wear a pointy hat? To keep his head warm—at least that's what it was for in the old days. Much like today, the popes of antiquity were elderly men who needed pro-

A: A *zucchetto*.

tection from the cold. So they wore simple cone-shaped hats, "the headgear of respectable men of the period," when they went outdoors. The hats didn't become purely ceremonial until much later.

Historical Note: The mitre started out as a short pointed cap, but by the twelfth century it had grown much taller and evolved from the closed cone shape into the open, two-pointed (one in front and one in back) version that popes wear today. The only difference: The popes of the twelfth century wore theirs *sideways*—with one point over each ear instead of in front and back like they do now. That created a problem: The points reminded people so much of the devil that they became known as horns . . . so the popes rotated their hats ninety degrees. They've worn them that way ever since.

THE ALB

Description: The floor-length white robe the priest wears over his street clothing during Mass.

Origin: The alb is a direct descendant of the Roman *tunic*, a shirt-like garment that reached all the way to the wearer's feet. Its name comes from *tunica alba*, which means "white tunic" in Latin.

THE CINCTURE

Description: The ropelike belt the priest uses to tie the alb around his waist.

Origin: Loose tunics were the mark of uncouth foreigners in the Roman Empire, where it was considered "slovenly, effeminate, and disrespectful" to wear a garment that wasn't gathered at the waist. People used just about anything as belts . . . even ropes.

THE STOLE

Description: The scarflike vestment the priest wears over the alb.

Origin: Magistrates and public officials of the Roman Empire wore stoles as a symbol of their authority. Priests wore them, too, after the empire converted to Christianity.

Four Eyes: Pope Leo X (1513-1521) was the first person in history to be

THE CHASUBLE

Description: The large outer garment the priest wears at Mass.

Origin: The chasuble was the raincoat of the Greco-Roman world. Today's version is shaped like a pancho—it's almost long enough to touch the floor in front and back but is short enough on the sides for the priest to stick his hands out. The original version was much more cumbersome: It was long all the way around, kind of like a skirt you wore around your neck, and had a hood. It got its name from *casula*, the Latin word for "little house," and was so bulky that a deacon had to stand behind the priest during Mass and gather the garment so that it wouldn't fall over his hands.

THE ROMAN COLLAR

Description: Nicknamed the "dog collar" because of its stiffness, the Roman collar is the standard street shirt for priests. (Only the white part is called the collar; the black part is called a "rabat.")

Origin: "Originally," says the Reverend Henry McCloud in his book *Clerical Dress and Insignia of the Roman Catholic Church*, the Roman collar "was nothing else than the shirt collar turned down over the cleric's everyday common dress in compliance with a fashion that began toward the end of the sixteenth century. For when the laity began to turn down their collars, the clergy also took up the mode."

. . . But that's only half the story: The clergy also adopted the fad of lining their collars with fancy lace and needlework, which made them more beautiful but also more difficult to clean. So a third custom arose: covering the collar with a changeable sleeve of white linen to protect it from dirt. The modest-minded Pope Urban VIII banned the use of lace in 1624 . . . but he didn't ban the protective sleeve. "Thus," McCloud says, "the narrow band of white linen used to protect the [collar] in the course of a few centuries became what is known today as the Roman collar."

depicted in art wearing concave-lens (nearsighted) eyeglasses.

CATHOLIC QUIZ #2
THE FLYING NUN

It was one of the most popular sitcoms of the late 1960s and has been a hit in syndication ever since . . . but how much do you remember about it? This quiz will help you find out.

A IR APPARENT
It was one of the most improbable sitcom plots in American television history: Elsie Ethrington, an American teenager, gives up her life as a beach bunny and enters a Puerto Rican nunnery called the Convent San Tanco, where she is professed as Sister Bertrille. Weighing only ninety pounds, she quickly discovers that wearing her order's bulky coronet (nun's hat) on windy days enables her to fly, a skill she uses to get into and out of trouble, fight crime, and occasionally assist the owner of a nearby casino.

. . . Sure, the *concept* was ridiculous, but the *show* was one of the surprise hits of the 1967 TV season. More importantly, it gave a needed boost to the acting career of nineteen-year-old actress Sally Field, who had just finished work on the *Gidget* TV series.

QUESTION TIME
How much do you remember about the show? Take the quiz below and find out. Answers are on page 198.

1. What was the inspiration for the show?

    (A) A real-life incident involving a small nun and a big hat.

    (B) A novel about a flying nun.

    (C) The TV shows *Bewitched* and *I Dream of Jeannie*.

    (D) All of the above.

Famous forgotten date: June 14, 1966, the day the *Index of Forbidden*

(E) Nun of the above: Sally Field came up with the idea herself.

2. The part of Sister Bertrille was custom-made for Sally Field ...but she turned it down when it was first offered to her. Why?

    (A) Fearful of scandal, the Vatican insisted that Field take a vow of chastity and keep it as long as she was on the show. She refused.

    (B) Field, herself a Catholic, had bad memories from her years in Catholic elementary and high schools . . . and didn't want to relive them.

    (C) Fresh from her beach bunny role as TV's *Gidget,* Field thought the role was too restrictive . . . and besides, she wanted to be a *movie* star, not a TV star.

3. What made her change her mind and take the role?

    (A) Her boyfriend dumped her to join the priesthood . . . and Field took the part in the hopes that dressing as a nun would help win him back.

    (B) Her movie career bit the dust.

    (C) Pope Paul VI, a big *Gidget* fan, phoned Field personally and urged her to take the role before studio executives offered it to Annette Funicello (the pope *hated* the *Mickey Mouse Club* TV show).

4. How did the other nuns on the show try to keep Sister Bertrille from flying?

    (A) Reverend Mother Plaseato (played by Madeline Sherwood) declared Sister Bertrille's flying powers a mortal sin . . . and forced her to go to confession after every flight. Bertrille spent so much time in confession after the first season that she hardly ever left the ground.

Books, first issued by Pope Paul IV in 1557, was finally abolished.

(B) They gave her a set of extra-heavy rosary beads.

(C) They tried to bulk her up with huge, heavy meals whenever possible and stuffed her pockets with holy cards, religious statues, and other items they found around the convent.

5. How did church officials respond to the show when it first went on the air?

(A) They condemned it out of hand.

(B) They refused to take a public stand.

(C) They liked it—and actually saw it as a recruiting film for nuns.

✠   ✠   ✠

. . . A SHORT-LIVED POPE'S SHORT STORY

What was Pope John Paul I (1978) like? A little tale he told during a papal audience before he died may provide a glimpse into his character.

"Once a man went to the car dealer to buy a car. The dealer told him: 'Look, the car is well equipped. Treat it well with premium gas and oil.'

"But the buyer said, 'No, I can't even stand the smell of gas and oil. I'll lubricate the engine with marmalade.'

" 'Do as you please,' said the dealer. 'But don't complain to me if you wind up in a ditch.'

"The Lord does something similar with us. He gave us these bodies enlivened with a soul and free will. He said, 'This mechanism is worth something; treat it well.' "

CONDEMNED!

*Did you know that the Catholic Church used to issue its own movie
ratings? It abandoned the practice in the early 1980s, but not before
classifying a number of modern film classics as "condemned" for
being "totally incompatible with Christian moral values."
Here are some review excerpts from the 1970s:*

National Lampoon's Animal House (1978)
"Too mindless to be satire, too unfunny to be farce, and too snide
and vicious to be likable. . . . Finally, besides being gross and vulgar in a variety of other ways, it exploits sex and nudity."

Midnight Express (1978)
"[Director Alan] Parker emphasizes the squalor, injustice, and bru-
tality. . . . His pictorial style wallows in violence, as soft focus and
closeups detail tortures, bloody brawls and horrid mutilations. All
this gore seems hardly justified by the human rights plea of
Midnight Express, a plea which is seriously weakened by its slurs on
the Turkish nation."

**Everything You Always Wanted to Know About Sex but Were
Afraid to Ask (Woody Allen, 1972)**
"What Allen has tried to do with the book—i.e., debunk it and its
creator and the lust-lusting public who bought it—is admittedly a
healthy pursuit. . . . But Allen as both comic and film maker
seems to fare better with sex-obsessed subjects than with the subject of sex itself. . . . In sum, Woody fails to do what possibly only
he could have done—to make a funny, intelligent spoof of an
inane, idiotic property."

Bananas (Woody Allen, 1971)
"Not too many people will 'go bananas' watching Woody Allen,
the nearsighted intellectual-buffoon, go through his familiar

First pontiff to fly in an airplane: Pope Paul VI (1963-1978) in 1964.

motions in this extended sit-com vehicle. . . . It is the standard picaresque Allen fare of tasteless insult and irreverence, chock full of gratuitous nonsense dragged in seemingly because there was still a little film in the camera. . . . The Catholics, for example, get theirs in a TV commercial which touts 'New Testament' cigarettes, which are offered to coughing communicants by a sympathetic priest. Such a sequence is calculated to offend anyone for whom religious belief is sacred."

Monty Python's Life of Brian (1980)

"The nihilistic, anything-for-a-laugh thrust of the film deliberately exploits much that is sacred to Christian tradition and to Jewish religious tradition as well. Especially offensive is the final crucifixion scene, which, with its unmistakable parallels to the Gospel story, comes across as a mocking parody of the Cross and Redemption of Christ."

Carrie (1976)

"If there were a Geiger counter-like instrument designed to detect traces of good taste and creative intelligence, one could run it over every square millimeter of Director Brian De Palma's latest effusion, a teenage horror show, without hearing the feeblest of beeps. . . . Sick humor, it seems, has become the last refuge of the slovenly, untalented filmmaker. . . . Beside the blood and gore, there is a good deal of crude sexual display and nudity."

Dirty Harry (1971)

"Before this film ends, the viewer is sated with the basic irresponsibility inherent in its voyeuristic, cynical superhero who . . . delights in sticking his .44-Magnum into a man's face and daring him to guess whether its chamber is empty. Detective or not, Harry [Clint Eastwood] is dangerous."

The 1784 New Hampshire Constitution had a religious test that forbade Catholics

LEGION OF DECENCY?

*You'd think that when a bunch of priests and religious laypeople get
together to censor films for the Catholic viewing public, they'd
condemn smutty blue movies and X-rated pornography out of
hand without watching each individual film, right? Think again.
Here are some of the more suspect films the National Catholic
Office for Motion Pictures (formerly known as the Legion of
Decency) sat and watched . . . so that we wouldn't have to.*

Deep Throat

The Bang Bang Gang

Hot Pants Holiday

Eroticon

Sex With a Smile

Tower of Screaming Virgins

Down and Dirty

Four Times That Night

Black Mama, White Mama

1000 Convicts and a Woman

Savage Sisters

Saturday Night at the Baths

Undercovers Hero

The Sensual Man

Flesh Gordon

Ann and Eve

Cindy and Donna

Cherry, Harry, and Raquel

Her and She and Him

Threesome

The Swappers

Women in Cellblock 7

Caged Men Plus One Woman

Chain Gang Women

Women in Revolt

The Brazen Women of Balzac

Night Call Nurses

Private Duty Nurses

The Student Nurses

The Sensuous Teenager

Teenage Sex Report

Jail Bait

Girls Are for Loving

The School Girls

Schoolgirls Growing Up

The House of Missing Girls

Weekend with the Babysitter

Trash

from running for office. They didn't obtain full civil liberties in the state until 1877.

MORE STRANGE SCENES

Some more examples of saints who are, in the words of one prominent archbishop, "lucky in faith, but unlucky in art."

SAINT HILARION (c. 291- c. 371)

How He's Portrayed: Naked and emaciated.

Reason: He was a devout desert hermit who wore almost nothing and was a big believer in religious fasts.

SAINT HEDWIG (c. 1174-1273)

How She's Portrayed: Barefoot, with her shoes under her arms.

Reason: Hedwig was a married woman who liked to go barefoot as a sign of humility—but her husband was so embarrassed by the spectacle that he bought her a pair of shoes and insisted that she never go out in public without them. Torn between religious conviction and her marriage vows, she compromised by interpreting her husband's instructions literally.

SAINT PETER MARTYR (c. 1205-1252)

How He's Portrayed: With a wound in his head or a dagger or knife cleaving his skull.

Reason: In 1252 Saint Peter and another Dominican friar were attacked by bandits while walking through the woods near Milan, Italy. Peter was stabbed in the chest and skull and killed. As he lay dying he prayed for his assassin and wrote the words "I believe in God" on the ground in his own blood, which so impressed the killer that he joined the Dominican order.

SAINT HIPPOLYTUS (c. 170- c. 235)

How He's Portrayed: Being dragged by horses.

Reason: Hippolytus was a Roman jailer in charge of guarding Saint Lawrence, a high official in the early Church who was later

Historians have described *Cooking Secrets of Pope Pius V,* first published in

martyred. Before he died, however, Lawrence converted
Hippolytus to Christianity—which so angered the Roman emper-
or Valerian that he had him tied behind two wild horses and
dragged across the countryside.

SAINT OSWALD (604-642)

How He Is Portrayed: Carrying his head on a sword.

Reason: An Anglo-Saxon king who converted his subjects to
Christianity, Saint Oswald was beheaded and dismembered after
he lost the battle of Maserfield in 642.

SAINT PELAGIA (c. 311)

How She Is Portrayed: Falling off a roof . . . or out of a window.

Reason: Some soldiers tried to rape her during the anti-Christian
persecutions of the Roman emperor Diocletian, but she had taken
a vow of chastity and was determined to reject their advances. So
she climbed up onto the roof of her house and either jumped or
fell into the sea when the soldiers followed her.

SAINT DYMPNA (c. 650)

How She's Portrayed: Being beheaded by a king . . . or in a
cloud, surrounded by lunatics chained with golden shackles.

Reason: According to legend, Dympna was the daughter of an
incestuous Celtic king who beheaded her after she ran away from
home. Over the centuries her grave developed a reputation for
curing sleepwalkers, epileptics, and mentally ill people who visited
it—so much so that she became the patron saint of the insane.

SAINT STANISLAUS (1030-1079)

How He's Portrayed: Being hacked to pieces in front of an altar.

Reason: Stanislaus, a Polish bishop, excommunicated King
Boleslaus the Cruel after he kidnapped the wife of a nobleman.
When the King found out, he stabbed Stanislaus to death,
chopped him into tiny pieces, and fed him to some wild animals.

1570, as "the most important and elaborate of the Renaissance cookbooks."

THE CADAVER SYNOD

We're used to thinking of the popes as holy men bursting at the seams with goodness and virtue. In truth, however, some of them were pretty evil. Take for example, Pope Stephen VI: He dug up the corpse of his predecessor, Pope Formosus I, dressed it in papal robes, and put it on trial for "aspiring to the papacy."

BACKGROUND. The ninth century A.D. was a difficult period in the history of the Catholic Church: The Holy Roman Empire, which had united all of western Europe under Emperor Charles the Great in 800, collapsed under the weight of Charles the Fat in 887. . . . and as the empire's power slipped away, so did the authority of the church: Not strong enough militarily to survive on its own, it had to turn to powerful (and often petty) European nobles for protection.

Desperate to save Rome from "pagans and evil Christians," in 889 Pope Stephen V lobbied King Arnulf of the eastern Franks to put the Eternal City under his protection. But Arnulf refused, forcing the pope to turn to an old enemy of the church, Duke Guido III of Spoleto, for protection. Guido agreed to come to Stephen's aid, and in return the Pope adopted him as his son and crowned him Holy Roman Emperor. (The *empire* had disintegrated, but European rulers still coveted the *title*).

POPE FORMOSUS

Not too long afterwards, Pope Stephen died and a new pope, Formosus I, was elected to head the church. But Guido was suspicious of Formosus's loyalty, so in 892 he forced the new pope to crown him emperor a second time and proclaim his son, Lambert of Spoleto, co-emperor and heir apparent. Formosus capitulated; but when Guido died in 894, rather than crown Lambert emperor, he called on King Arnulf to liberate Rome from the Spoletans. This time Arnulf agreed: A year later he conquered Rome and was crowned Holy Roman Emperor instead of Lambert, who had retreated back to Spoleto.

Bad Luck
The new order didn't last long. A few months later Arnulf became paralyzed and was carried back to Germany on a stretcher, where he later died. Pope Formosus died in April 896 and a longtime rival, Stephen VI, was elected pope in his place. When Lambert of Spoleto learned of the deaths, he rallied his troops and marched on the city, conquering it in 897. Pope Stephen crowned him emperor a few days later.

TRIAL AND PUNISHMENT
What followed was one of the most peculiar episodes in the history of the Catholic Church. Eager to prove his loyalty to Lambert, Pope Stephen convened what would become known as the Cadaver Synod: On his orders Pope Formosus's rotting nine-month-old corpse was dug up, dressed in papal robes, propped up on a throne . . . and put on trial for perjury, coveting the papacy, and a variety of other crimes. (Since Formosus was in no condition to answer the charges made against him, Stephen appointed a deacon to stand next to his corpse during the proceedings and answer questions on its behalf.)

The deacon mounted an impressive defense; even so, the cadaver was found guilty on all counts. Stephen declared all of Formosus's papal acts null and void and chopped off the three fingers on the corpse's right used to give blessings; then he had the body stripped naked and dumped in a cemetery for foreigners. A few days later he had the corpse dug up and flung into the Tiber River, where a hermit fished it out and gave it a proper burial.

What Goes Around . . .
Stephen survived the Cadaver Synod by only a few months: While the gruesome proceedings were still in session, a strong earthquake struck Rome and destroyed the papal basilica. Taking this as a sign of God's anger with Stephen VI (and encouraged by

A. The Apostles' Creed.

rumors that Formosus's corpse had begun performing miracles), Formosus's supporters arrested Stephen and threw him into prison, where he was later strangled.

PROS AND CONS

. . . But the story doesn't end there: The Cadaver Synod ignited a power struggle between supporters of Formosus and Stephen that lasted for more than ten years and cost at least one other pope his life. How bitter was the struggle? See for yourself.:

POPE ROMANUS I (August-November 897). A pro-Formosus cardinal, Romanus served as pope for only four months. According to church records, "he was afterwards made a monk," which is a polite way of saying he was deposed and imprisoned in a monastery. His date and cause of death are unknown.

POPE THEODORE II (November-December 897). Another supporter of Formosus; he died of unknown causes after only twenty days in office. During that short time he had Formosus's body reburied in its original grave and presided over a synod renouncing the Cadaver Synod.

POPE SERGIUS III (December 897). A pro-Stephen pope, Sergius planned to call a synod to renounce Pope Theodore's synod renouncing the Cadaver Synod, but Lambert of Spoleto forced him into exile before he got the chance. (See below.)

POPE JOHN IX (January 898-January 900). The next pope, John IX, was pro-Lambert—but he was also pro-Formosus, and not long after becoming pope he convened his own synod condemning the Cadaver Synod; then he called a *second* synod to ratify the decisions of his first synod. He also issued a decree prohibiting the trial of dead people, especially popes.

POPE BENEDICT IV (May 900-August 903). Yet another Formosan pope, Benedict called his own synod and again condemned the Cadaver Synod. He died of mysterious causes in 903; rumor has it he was murdered.

POPE LEO V (August-September 903). The third pro-Formosus pope in a row, Leo ruled for only thirty days (apparently not enough time to call a synod) before he was overthrown and imprisoned by the antipope Christopher, who was himself overthrown three months later.

POPE SERGIUS III (904-911). With the assistance of Duke Alberic of Spoleto, in 904 Pope Sergius III (see above) returned from exile and conquered Rome. He deposed the antipope Christopher and threw him into prison with Pope Leo V; he later had both men strangled. Then he (of course) convened a synod, which he used to condemn Theodore's, John's, and Benedict's synods and restate the Cadaver Synod. He died in April 911.

✠ ✠ ✠

. . . CATHOLIC PARENT ALERT!
Ever wonder who's corrupting our Catholic youth? Here's one theory:

> Once the restraining influence of school has gone, the adolescent realizes he can mix with anybody and it is very difficult for his parents to prevent any friendships that he may wish to make. . . . Simon, for instance, leaves school to work in a factory, where his wages, as an apprentice, seem very small for all that he wants to do. He feels that Mike, a Communist, has really "got something" with his talk of equal rights for all workers and "down with the Capitalists." Added to this, Mike's sandals, hectically colored shirt and general unkemptness have all the attraction of novelty, his loud and unrestricted speech drowns all arguments by its very fluency and his beard goes a long way towards showing his virility and maturity. "And what," Simon persuades himself, "could be more truly Christian than a doctrine of equality for all?" If his depth of belief in, and his knowledge of, the true Faith are not great, he will soon be talked into that frame of mind which will accept, ultimately, the Communist views on "free love," the "bourgeois" habit of church going, and the totalitarianism of Papal rule from the Vatican.
>
> *A Catholic Parent's Guide to Sex Education,* 1962

On average, 47 Bibles per minute are sold or distributed around the world every day.

COMING TO AMERICA

Every papal trip is planned to the tiniest detail, but not everything goes according to plan—and the trips aren't popular with everyone. Here's a look at Pope John Paul II's trip to Denver, Colorado, in August 1993 for the church's World Youth Day celebrations.

MONDAY, AUGUST 9, 1993
12:54 P.M.: The pope's special Alitalia Boeing 747 arrives in Kingston, Jamaica, where he stops over for a two-day official visit. His visit is protested by "Protestants and reggae singers," who charge that he is a symbol of Jamaica's colonial past; and by the poor of Kingston, who complain that the only potholes and water mains being fixed on the island are the ones along the pontiff's parade route.

Meanwhile, back in the U.S.: A nationwide shortage of Porta Potties begins as thousands of the "comfort stations" are trucked to Denver for World Youth Day. The shortage is particularly acute in the Midwest, where record flooding has knocked out plumbing in several major cities. "We were told we would have 5,000 Porta Potties by 6 P.M. Tuesday," complains Des Moines police chief Nicholas Brown. "Instead we got none. We found out that most of the Porta Potties were being sent to Denver because of the pope's visit."

WEDNESDAY, AUGUST 11
8:00 A.M.: An estimated 186,000 young Catholics from seventy-two different countries descend upon Denver, Colorado, to celebrate the Catholic Church's eighth annual World Youth Day. Hotels are booked solid, forcing thousands of youths to look for other accommodations. Eighty-five hundred end up sleeping in cattle stalls at Denver's National Western Stock Show building; fifteen hundred more pitch their tents in a downtown parking garage. A sense of camaraderie develops among the inhabitants—

Famous forgotten Catholic: John Philip Holland, inventor of the submarine.

locals warn foreigners and out-of-towners not to wear blue or red clothing so they won't get shot by Denver street gangs.

THURSDAY, AUGUST 12
2:30 P.M.: Pope John Paul II arrives at Denver's Stapleton Airport to cheers of "John Paul Two, we love you!" and is greeted by President Clinton. Later he travels to Mile High Stadium, circles the playing field in his popemobile, and is welcomed by throngs of World Youth Day participants. He addresses the crowd; afterwards ninety thousand youths—and at least a hundred bishops—do "the wave."

FRIDAY, AUGUST 13
That afternoon: Journalists complain they are denied access to the pope. "The press is driving me nuts," says Sister Mary Ann Walsh, the official spokeswoman (and the person who issued thirty-five hundred press credentials to reporters). "I don't think it's fair to use an event that's been planned and developed for and by young people to grab media attention."

Later that afternoon: The pope grants an official interview . . . to a team of eight-year-old "reporters." One question he fields: whether or not he has ever hit anyone on the head while swinging his *censer* (incense container). Rather than dodge the question, he tackles it head-on. "So far I have never hit anyone in the head with the censer," he tells the tykes.

SATURDAY, AUGUST 14
8 A.M.: An estimated twenty thousand World Youth Day participants begin a fourteen-mile pilgrimage to Cherry Creek State Park outside Denver. During the trek their numbers swell to sixty thousand.

11:00 A.M.: The mile-high altitude, scorching sun, and eighty-degree heat take their toll on the marchers. "All the first aid stations are reporting overload conditions," the sheriff's department spokesman tells the press. "They are calling for IV supplies and additional medical personnel." Six thousand people seek help from emergency medical crews; 150 serious cases are taken to local hospitals. "It was an amazing sight," one state official told reporters. "It was a continuous stream of people coming in with various injuries, dehydration, and sprains." One man dies from a heart attack.

Still, not everyone is suffering; one team of elderly nuns from Mexico City finishes the hike without any problems. Group leader Sister Rosa Maria Gomez describes it as *"nada"*—nothing. She recalls a similar trek in 1979: "We went on our knees across the plaza to our allotted seats. But we were younger then and not so fat."

Saturday evening: The National Weather Service predicts temperatures for Sunday will hit the mid-eighties. (They will actually climb into the nineties). Church and state officials, worried about the outdoor Mass planned for the following morning, double the number of paramedics at the site and order extra IV solution brought in on tractor-trailer trucks. The sheriff takes to the airwaves urging the elderly and the sick to stay away. "If you're not accustomed to these conditions," he warns the public, "stay home and watch it on TV. That's the best way to see it all and stay healthy."

Saturday night: The overnight temperature at the pilgrimage campside drops into the mid-fifties. The altitude and chilly weather take their toll on the faithful; after suffering all day in the heat, an estimated five hundred campers seek medical attention, complaining of the cold.

SUNDAY, AUGUST 15
9:30 A.M.: The outdoor papal Mass at Cherry Creek State Park begins. An estimated 375,000 people, including 250,000 worshippers who camped out at the sight overnight, are in attendance. Topic for the pope's sermon: "the culture of death." He lumps

At one of the many orgies he hosted, Pope Alexander VI (1492-1503) gave prizes to together the issues of birth control, abortion, euthanasia, alcohol abuse, pornography, and violence. According to the Associated Press, the sermon contains "some of the strongest rhetoric of his 15-year papacy." To make his message clear, the pope delivers portions of it in English, French, Italian, and Spanish.

Approximately 10:30 A.M.: A very different culture of death descends upon the three-and-a-half-hour Mass as the altitude, scorching sun, and temperatures in the nineties decimate the hundreds of thousands of unprepared faithful cramming the shadeless, 120-acre site. Many beg for water. Hundreds of containers are distributed into the crowd from the altar, and vendors in the back sell pints of water for two dollars a bottle. But none of it makes it to the center of the crowd, where Catholics are really suffering. The fire department sprays the sufferers with fire hoses as Mass continues undisturbed.

About 11:00 A.M.: The situation deteriorates as the temperature continues to climb. "Everybody's passing out up front," one sixteen-year-old tells reporters. "They're dropping like flies." Paramedics and volunteers use stretchers, sleeping bags, and anything else that will work to carry thousands of semiconscious and unconscious celebrants to the first aid stations ringing the site. Serious cases are taken to a field hospital set up nearby.

Making matters worse, participants aren't as helpful as they could be: According the *Los Angeles Times*, "Many in the crowd were mystified that the Mass participants seemed oblivious to the suffering around them. At one point during the 3-1/2 hour Mass, paramedics pleaded for a parade of 20 white-robed priests serving Communion to move from the path of emergency vehicles ferrying stricken worshippers."

Approximately 11:30 A.M.: Tent clinics set up at the Mass site are overwhelmed as more than fourteen thousand celebrants request medical attention. Ambulances ferrying the worst cases to the field hospital are so backlogged that it takes more than fifteen minutes to unload patients; and there aren't enough beds for the

the men "who copulated the most times" with the papal prostitutes.

masses of people needing attention. The remaining sick are tended to on the sidewalk, where they are covered with blankets to protect them from the sun. One thirty-one-year-old woman goes into critical condition after suffering a series of seizures. (She later recovers.)

1:00 P.M.: The papal mass ends . . . and the fingerpointing begins, as church, state, and medical officials look for someone to blame for the calamities of the past two days. One paramedic blames the church. "It was a war zone—to say that we were overwhelmed is an overstatement. I think World Youth Day owes a big apology to the medical community and its own participants." Nonsense, says Sister Mary Ann Walsh, communications director of the event, who blames the participants themselves. "I wish that 2 percent of the young people had not had their wonderful experience marred by succumbing to the heat," she told reporters. "You can lead the youth to water, but you can't make them drink."

Late Sunday afternoon: A driving rainstorm pummels the ten thousand faithful who have not yet left the Mass site.

MONDAY, AUGUST 16
9:00 A.M.: A small army of Denver sanitation workers begin removing approximately forty tons of garbage—including plastic tarps, bottles, and lawn furniture left behind by the faithful—from the Mass site. The job will take about two days—but environmentalists estimate it will take about three years for the parkland to return to its natural state.

Later in the day: Small business owners tally up receipts for the weekend and arrive at a conclusion: The Youth Day crowd was extremely tightfisted. As the *New York Times* put it, "The young Catholics came to Denver with the Ten Commandments and a $10 bill—and they're determined not to break either one."

7:15 P.M.: John Paul II returns to Rome on *Shepherd One*, a modified Boeing 767. The trip is no ordinary flight: The pope will sleep

William "Buffalo Bill" Cody (1846-1917) was Catholic.

in a custom-made bed (complete with specially ordered Belgian sheets, embroidered pillowcases, a down comforter, and a curtained enclosure) in the first-class compartment. On the dinner menu: caviar and a choice of beef, chicken, veal, or salmon with linguine, with ice cream sundaes and chocolates for dessert. Per the pope's special request, cake is also served.

✠ ✠ ✠

. . . STILL, IT COULD HAVE BEEN WORSE

Here's what happened to the pope when he visited the Netherlands in May 1985:

> When Pope John Paul II takes to the road, crowds are almost always huge and the mood celebratory. The Pontiff's magical spell, however, was abruptly snapped in the Netherlands last week. . . . The Dutch, with 5.6 million Roman Catholics among 14.5 million citizens, accorded John Paul a remarkably unfriendly reception. . . . The ugliest episode began in Utrecht with protesters who had assembled under a legal permit. Several dozens of the 1,000 marchers sang, "We're going to kill, kill, kill the Pope tonight" while pelting police with rocks, bottles, and smoke bombs. At one point, a bottle, cans, and eggs were hurled toward the bulletproof white Popemobile. . . . Was the trip to the Netherlands worth the risk? Papal advisers put the best face on things, insisting that John Paul knew all along that local conditions would make the visit difficult. Said one member of his entourage, "Everyone is happy there was no real disaster."
>
> —*Time* magazine, May 27, 1985

"Prelate" comes from the Latin word *praeferre*, which means "to prefer to another."

POPE JUNK

Some unusual gift suggestions for the Catholic who has everything.

TACKY, TACKY, TACKY...
They're as familiar a part of papal visits as the popemobile itself—whenever the Pope travels to the United States (or anywhere, for that matter), hucksters try to cash in on the event by dreaming up pope souvenirs. "I know people kind of look at us like we're the moneychangers outside the temple," says Patrick Moran, one pope-preneur, "but I draw a distinction between Jesus and the pope. The pope is fair game." Today even the Catholic Church *itself* sells souvenirs during papal visits. It started when John Paul II visited the United States in August 1993. Why? To help defray the huge cost of the papal visit and also to squelch tasteless unofficial souvenirs, the Church says. "The things that everybody laughs at, we didn't want to be associated with," says Sister Mary Ann Walsh, spokesperson for the pope's September 1993 visit to Denver. "We want to avoid tastelessness." Not everyone does, though, as these products demonstrate:

Pope Rug. After Pope John Paul II celebrated Mass in Denver, Colorado, Dennis Bylina bought some of the carpet the pontiff stood upon during the service and started selling it to the public in one-square-inch pieces for three dollars apiece. (He paid eight dollars a *yard* for the carpet.) Church officials condemned the project. "I'm gravely doubtful of its legitimacy and the prudence of this," said a spokesperson for the Denver archdiocese. "It demeans the experience." Nonsense, says Bylina. "The church was selling T-shirts and mugs and everything else with the pope on them."

Pope-on-a-Rope Soap. The original classic: For about ten dollars, you can bathe with a smaller, soapier version of the Holy Father. (The company's motto: "Wash away your sins.")

Pope Watch. Like a Mickey Mouse watch, only holier.

Dominican monks used to be known as the "watchdogs of the Lord."

Let Us Spray Lawn Sprinkler. Shaped like Pope John Paul II, the sprinkler squirts water out of his outstretched arms as it spins.

Pope Kiss Ring. A three-dollar fake gold ring with plastic lips (supposedly the pope's) that kiss back when you kiss them.

Pope Fan. Has a picture of the pope on it (of course) and the slogan "I am a fan of Pope John Paul II."

Pope/Beatles T-shirt. Has three people on it: George, Ringo . . . and John Paul.

OTHER CATHOLIC PRODUCTS
These items should still be available:

Jesus: The Doll. Invented by Nancy Pulte Rickard, who was looking for a way to help children discover Jesus and was inspired to make the doll after visiting Medjugorje. "One of the big things about the doll," she says, "is it makes it hard for people to deny his presence. They look across the a room and go, 'Oh, there's Jesus.' " This machine-washable version of the savior is about two feet tall and wears a red robe with a white tunic underneath it. Call 800-227-8702 for more information.

The Rosary Tapes. Puts the rosary to contemporary music (including classical, jazz, light rock, country and western, and gospel) so that you can say the rosary in your car. One tape each for the joyful, sorrowful, and glorious mysteries. Write to The Rosary Tapes, P.O. Box 6037, Saginaw, MI 48608-6037 for more information.

The Fighting Nun. A small boxing puppet that looks like a nun. (The company's slogan: "She's got a habit . . . fighting for what's right!") Available from Accoutrements, P.O. Box 30811, Seattle, WA 98103.

Pope Rosary. Has a centerpiece with Pope John Paul II on it, and a picture of a Roman basilica on each Our Father bead. Available from the Leaflet Missal Company, 976 West Minnehaha Ave., St. Paul, MN 55104-1556.

Wanna bet? London bookies have pegged the odds of a future female pope at 1,000 to 1.

GIRL TROUBLE

*If you think today's church is male-dominated,
you should have seen it in the old days:*

"Adam was led to sin by Eve and not Eve by Adam. It is just and right that woman accept as lord and master him whom she led to sin."
—Saint Ambrose (334-397)

"The woman, together with her own husband, is the image of God . . . but when she is referred to separately . . . the woman alone, then she is not the image of God, but as regards the man alone, he is the image of God."
—Saint Augustine (354-430)

"Woman—a foe to friendship, an inescapable punishment, a necessary evil."
—Saint John Chrysostom (347-407)

"Married life presupposes the power of the husband over the wife and children, and the subjection and obedience of the wife to the husband."
—Pope Pius XI (1922-1939)

"Among savage beasts none is found so harmful as a woman."
—Saint John Chrysostom

"When you see a woman, consider that you face not a human being, but the devil himself. The woman's voice is the hiss of the snake."
—Saint Anthony (1195-1231)

"[Woman is] carnal and sensuous, [the] irrational half of mankind."
—Saint Methodius (c. 310)

"Woman is naive, unstable, mentally weak, and in need of an authoritative husband."
—Pope Saint Gregory (540-604)

"Woman's philosophy is to obey the laws of marriage. . . . Let the house be thy city."
—Saint Gregory of Nazianzus

Pope Dope: Pope Leo XIII (1878-1903) regularly drank Mariani wine, which

MYTH-UNDERSTOOD?
THE BIRTH OF JESUS

If you're a stickler for authenticity, you might want to think twice about unpacking your nativity scene this Christmas . . . because according to modern scholars, just about everything it depicts is inaccurate.

THE FIRST NOEL

Picture a nativity scene: Mary and Joseph are kneeling in a stable alongside the baby Jesus, who is lying in an animal trough filled with straw. The three kings of the Orient—Caspar, Balthasar, and Melchior—are in the foreground; so are some shepherds. They in turn are surrounded by cows, sheep, camels, donkeys, horses . . .

How much of this scene is accurate? Was Jesus *really* born in a stable? Did Mary lay him in a bed of straw? Was the place crawling with livestock? No—at least that's what most historians and Bible scholars say. The gospels of the New Testament, the only original sources of information on the nativity, don't mention any of these details. They don't say much at all, for that matter: Matthew says simply that "Jesus was born in Bethlehem" and skips straight to the wise men; Luke says only that Mary "gave birth to her firstborn son and wrapped him in swaddling cloths, and laid him in a manger, because there was no place for them at the inn," and moves immediately to the shepherds who came to visit. That's all there is—Mark and John skip the birth scene entirely.

Where do we get the rest of our information? From generations of well-meaning Christians, who over the centuries have embellished the gospel accounts with details based on their understanding of life in Bethlehem in the first century A.D. The only problem: They were almost completely ignorant of life in first-century Bethlehem—and nearly all of the details they added are untrue. Here's what many experts speculate may really have happened:

is made from the same plant from which cocaine is extracted.

• **Mary gave birth without Joseph.** There may have been mid-wives and other women present, but there certainly weren't any men there . . . not even Joseph. Religious law and social customs forbade the presence of men.

• **She was probably only fourteen to sixteen years old.** That was the age at which young girls married in the ancient world; it would have been extremely unusual for her to be any older than that. Mary was certainly nowhere near as old she is most often depicted, which is mid- to late twenties or early thirties.

• **She probably gave birth in a house.** The Greek word for "inn" can also be translated "house," "guest house," or "room"—and many historians consider "house" or "room" to be a more accurate translation than "inn." Reason: They speculate that Joseph, who was from Bethlehem, had relatives there—and since he was trav-eling with his pregnant wife, he would have stayed with them instead of in a hotel.

  If Mary and Joseph didn't sleep in a stable *or* an inn, and the house or room was full as it says in the Bible, where did they sleep? One theory: In the ground-floor room of a typical two-story Bethlehem dwelling. Such rooms were typically used for storage and would have been available in a pinch even if the upstairs rooms were full. That may have been what Luke meant: The *bed-rooms* were full, so Mary and Joseph slept downstairs. But that's just one theory: Other scholars believe Mary gave birth in a cave.

• **She didn't give birth in an animal trough . . . or lay Jesus in one afterwards.** "The word 'manger' carried a range of meanings," many of which had nothing to do with animals, says Brent Walters, an expert on first-century church history. "What mother is going to give birth in an animal's trough? . . . Are you going to lay a brand-new baby with open eyes, ears, nose and mouth onto chopped hay, which is going to pierce the flesh and which is filthy from animals being about? . . . These people knew something about sanitation."

The Great Salt Cathedral, made entirely of salt, is located 800 feet underground in the

- **There weren't any animals present.** "There are no animals mentioned in the story itself," says John Elliott, a theologian and expert on first-century Palestine. "Jesus was born in something that was translated as 'manger' or 'animal trough,' and the assumption is made there were animals feeding there. So you pack the creche with a few animals."

Even if Mary had *wanted* to give birth in a stable, she probably wouldn't have been able to. Hardly anyone in Bethlehem had them: The weather was mild enough that animals slept outside most of the year; and on really cold nights they could be quartered in the ground-floor storage room.

- **The "three kings" weren't kings—and there were more than three of them . . . *a lot more*.** "Nowhere in the texts does it say there were three of them; nowhere does it say they were kings," Elliott says. "Over the centuries, we've come to give them names: Caspar, Balthasar and Melchior; but that's not mentioned either."

Who were they? The Greek text of Matthew describes them not as kings but as *magoi*. "These were astrologers, scholars and philosophers," Walters reports, "and there would have been at least 40 magi, because they traveled in groups of that size." The Bible doesn't give a specific number of magi—so why does tradition say there were only three? One theory: Matthew says they brought three gifts, gold, frankincense, and myrrh . . . and at some point in history, people assumed that there was one person for each gift.

- **If there really were shepherds there, they were most likely smelly, dirty . . . and vulgar.** They were the first-century equivalent of Hell's Angels or used-car salesmen: Everyone hated them. "Shepherds were real outcasts whom the Palestinians dreaded seeing," Elliott says. "They were migrants, they had no roots, they were not respected because they never stayed in one place long enough to develop any loyalties. They smelled bad, and their animals trampled crops. They were not only uncouth, but they were on the absolute margins of society." What were they doing there

world's largest active salt mine in Zipaquira, Columbia. It seats almost 5,000 people.

in the first place? Elliot believes they were there (or that Luke *put* them there) for three reasons: To show that Jesus was the Messiah for *all* people, even the absolute dregs of society; to anticipate Jesus' later descriptions of himself as a shepherd of men; and to link him with the house of David, a shepherd who became king.

✠ ✠ ✠

. . . NEWS ITEMS

"Madrid, Spain: Four Colombian men were arrested after police seized a 12-figure nativity scene filled with cocaine worth $2 million. . . . Agents found 6.6 pounds of the drug inside statues of the baby Jesus, the Virgin Mary, the three kings and little lambs."

—Newspaper report, December 25, 1988

"Desk-top Virgin Sparks Cop Feud. Lynn, Massachusetts: Two police commanders feuding over a 9-inch statuette of the Virgin Mary on their shared desk have been put on different shifts, but their dispute continues. . . . The fight started when Capt. Bruce Hogan placed the pale yellow Madonna on the desk they shared. . . . Hogan accused Lt. Eugene Begley, his desk partner, of shrouding the religious icon in newspaper and skirting his order not to touch it. 'I never touched it,' Begley told reporters. 'I just put the cup over it.' On Tuesday, a state arbitrator heard Begley's claim that the shift transfer has cost him $45,000 annually in pay for extra assignments. Three more hearings are scheduled."

—The *San Jose Mercury News*, January 26, 1989

"Alba, Italy: A group of Italian nuns seeking new recruits are offering women an expenses-paid weekend in a convent—and hoping some will stay. The 43 Dominican sisters of the convent in northern Italy put advertisements in local newspapers offering the free weekend."

—Wire report, July 28, 1989

Pope Clement VII (1478-1534) died from eating poison mushrooms.

IT'S GREEK TO ME

*You know that the church is Roman Catholic . . . but did
you know that it gets a lot of its words from the Greeks?
Here are some examples . . .*

Apostle: From the Greek word *apostolos*, which means "one sent out."

Bible: From *byblos*, the word for "papyrus." (Early paper was made from papyrus.)

Christ: A translation of the Hebrew word *meshia*, which means "anointed one."

Church: From *kyriakon*, meaning "the Lord's house."

Devil: From *diabolos*, which means "slanderer."

Angel: From *angelos*, the Greek word for "herald" or "messenger."

Pope: From the Greek word *pappas* (and the Latin word *papa*), meaning "father."

Hermit: From *eremites*, which means "man of the desert."

Monk, monastery: Both come from *monos*, the Greek word for "alone."

Orthodox: From the words *orthos* and *doxa*, which mean "right opinion."

Heterodox: Means "other opinion."

Bishop: From *episkopos*, which means "overseer."

Cleric: From *kleros*, which means "heritage."

Laity: From *laos*, which means "the people."

Agnostic: From *agnostos*, the Greek word for "unknowable." (The word was coined by Thomas Huxley, a nineteenth-century English biologist, during a dinner party in 1869.)

Baptize: From *baptizo*, which means "immerse."

Paradise: From *paradeisos*, the Greek word for "park."

Hierarchy: From the Greek word *hierarchia*, which means "holy rule."

Amen is a Hebrew word that can mean "certainly," "truly,"—and even "So be it."

IT'S A MIRACLE!

The saints are remembered most for their holy deeds, but many of them are also credited with having legendary powers. Here are some of the stranger ones:

Saint Hugh of Grenoble (1052-1132). Made the sign of the cross over some chickens and turned them into sea turtles, so that some hungry monks could eat them on a meatless Friday (sea turtles were considered fish).

Saint Nicholas of Tolentino (1245-1305). A similar story—rather than break a religious fast, Nicholas made the sign of the cross over a bird that someone had cooked for him; it sprang to life and flew away.

Saint Leufredus (c. 738). Struck bald a woman who made fun of his baldness; struck toothless a thief who had slandered him; and struck infertile the fields of a farmer who had plowed on Sunday. Also banished the flies from his house one afternoon when they interrupted his prayers; for this reason he is the patron saint invoked against flies.

Saint Brigid (c. 450-525). Hung her wet laundry on sunbeams, taught a fox to dance, and changed her dirty bathwater into beer so that visiting clerics would have something to drink.

Saint Peter Martyr (1205-1252). Cursed some young hoodlums who were throwing stones at a building. The building collapsed on the boys, killing them.

Saint Fillian (eighth century). His left arm glowed so brightly he could read by it at night.

Saint Gwen (seventh century). Grew a third breast after giving birth to triplets (in honor of the Trinity).

The Nixon Pope? Acting on the instructions of Pope Pius XII (1939-1958), the

Saint Lawrence (third century). Leads one soul out of purgatory every Friday (not to be confused with Saint Patrick, who leads seven souls out of purgatory each Thursday and twelve each Saturday).

Saint Joseph of Cupertino (1603-1663). Could recognize sinners "because their faces appeared black to him," and could spot "perverts and sexual offenders" because they gave off a foul stench.

Saint Fridolin (c. 650). Had X-ray vision . . . or at least could see through the rubble of a monastery at Poiters, where he found the remains of Saint Hilary (patron saint of lawyers and backward children).

Saint Blaise (c 275). Talked a wolf into giving back a pig it had stolen.

Saint Francis of Assisi (c. 1181-1226). Also good with animals. On one occasion he "preached a sermon to the birds"; on another he "made a peace treaty with a wolf."

Saint Martin de Porres (1579-1639). Could levitate and "bilocate" (appear in two places at once) and glowed in the dark when he prayed.

Saint Antony of Padua (1195-1231). Reattached the leg of a guilt-ridden young man who had cut it off after kicking his mother with it.

Saint Peter Martyr (1205-1252). *Told* a young man to chop off his foot after he kicked his mother . . . and then reattached it after the young man obeyed the order.

Saint Eligius (c. 590- c. 660). Tried to nail a horseshoe on the hoof of a restless horse, but the animal was so fidgety that he had to saw off its leg to do it. He reattached it afterwards by "making the sign of the cross over it, so that no trace of a wound could be seen."

papal police regularly tapped the Vatican City's phone lines.

THE ONE TRUE FAITH

*Is Roman Catholicism the only true religion? You betcha—
at least according to Church teachings before Vatican II.
Here are some more excerpts from the* Baltimore Catechism #3.

Q. 516. Why can there be only one true religion?
A. There can be only one true religion, because a thing cannot be
false and true at the same time, and, therefore, all religions that
contradict the teaching of the true Church must teach falsehood.
If all religions in which men seek to serve God are equally good
and true, why did Christ disturb the Jewish religion and the
Apostles condemn heretics?

Q. 509. Are all bound to belong to the Church?
A. All are bound to belong to the Church, and he who knows the
Church to be the true Church and remains out of it cannot be
saved.

**Q. 514. What excuses do some give for not becoming members
of the true Church?**
A. The excuses some give . . . are: (1) They do not wish to leave
the religion in which they were born; (2) there are too many poor
and ignorant people in the Catholic Church; (3) one religion is as
good as another if we try to serve God in it, and be upright and
honest and upright in our lives.

Q. 515. How do you answer such questions?
A. (1) To say that we should remain in a false religion because we
were born in it is as untrue as to say we should not heal our bodily
diseases because we were born with them; (2) to say there are too
many poor and ignorant in the Catholic Church is to declare that
it is Christ's Church; for He always taught the poor and ignorant
and instructed His Church to continue the work; (3) to say that

Q: Why is St. Vincent—a teetotaler—the patron saint of wine?

one religion is as good as another is to assert that Christ labored uselessly and taught falsely; for He came to abolish the old religion and found the new in which alone we can be saved as He Himself declared.

Q. 554. Could a person who denies only one article of our faith be a Catholic?
A. A person who denies even one article of our faith could not be a Catholic; for truth is one and we must accept it whole and entire or not at all.

Q. 1169. Who are they who do not believe all God has taught?
A. They who do not believe all that God has taught are the heretics and infidels. . . . The denial of only one article of faith will make a person a heretic and guilty of mortal sin, because the Holy Scripture says: "Whosoever shall keep the whole law but offend in one point is become guilty of all."

Q. 1179. Can they who fail to profess their faith in the true Church in which they believe expect to be saved while in that state?
A. They who fail to profess their faith in the true Church in which they believe cannot expect to be saved while in that state, for Christ has said: "Whosoever shall deny me before men, I will also deny him before my Father who is in heaven."

Q. 510. Is it ever possible for one to be saved who does not know the Catholic Church to be the true Church?
A. It is possible . . . provided that person (1) has been validly baptized; (2) firmly believes the religion he professes and practices to be the true religion; and (3) dies without the guilt of mortal sin on his soul. . . . Such persons are said to belong to the "soul of the Church"; that is, they are really members of the Church without knowing it. Those who share in its Sacraments and worship are said to belong to the body or visible part of the Church.

A: His last name begins with *vin.*

ADOLF HITLER, LAPSED CATHOLIC

Did you know Hitler was baptized a Catholic? As an adult, he set out to destroy the Catholic Church . . . but as a boy, he sang in the choir. Here are some things you probably never knew about him.

He literally owed his life to the Vatican. Hitler's parents were second cousins—at least on paper. His father, Alois Schicklgruber, was an illegitimate child who in 1876 falsely testified to church officials that his was father Johann Georg Hitler (originally spelled "Hiedler"), a family friend. This created problems in 1884 when Alois tried to marry Klara Pözl, a Hitler relative. Church law forbade marriages between cousins, and the Vatican itself had to grant a special dispensation before the couple could wed. It did so in January of 1885; the Hitlers were married a few days later. Klara gave birth to Adolf in 1889.

• **He went to Catholic school.** Hitler's family lived across the street from the Benedictine monastery in Lambach, Austria, and eight-year-old Adolf started school there in 1897. According to biographer Robert Payne in his book *The Life and Death of Adolf Hitler*, he loved it. "Adolf . . . was immediately fascinated by the new world of church ritual, the black-robed monks, the abbot ruling his flock with all the authority of an earthly king. . . . In his spare time he took singing lessons so he could sing in the choir."

• **He encountered his first swastikas *at church*.** The Lambach monastery had several swastikas on its grounds, including one that was clearly visible from the Hitler family apartment. The symbol (which originally symbolized *good* luck) was part of the coat of arms of Abbot Theodorich von Hagen, who ran the monastery in the 1850s. Payne and other historians speculate that these swastikas were the inspiration for the Nazi symbol years later.

Two slivers of wood, purportedly taken from the cross on which

Historical Note: Why did von Hagen decorate the monastery with swastikas? Some historians believe he did it as a pun on his last name: The German word for swastika, *Hakenkreuz* ("hooked cross"), is only one letter different from "Hagen's cross," *Hagenkreuz*.

• **He wanted to become a priest . . . at least at first.** Frau Helene Hanfstangel, the wife of one of Hitler's cronies, recalled Hitler telling her that "as a small boy it was his most ardent wish to become a priest. He often borrowed the large kitchen apron of his maid, climbed on a kitchen chair and delivered long and fervent sermons." Payne notes that "for two years Adolf contemplated the possibility of one day joining the community of monks, eventually rising to the position of abbot, with supreme authority over all the monks."

• **What caused Hitler to lose his interest in religious life?** Historians point to a childhood run-in with a parish priest as the possible answer. "One day, when [Hitler] was about nine years old, a priest caught him smoking a cigarette. This was a serious matter, and for a while he was in danger of receiving exemplary punishment. The danger passed, for the priest quickly forgave him, and he resumed his schooling as though nothing had happened." Even so, Hitler never forgot the incident (and for that matter never took up smoking); Payne and others point to it as the possible beginning of his break from the Catholic Church.

By the time he was confirmed at the age of fourteen in 1904, Hitler's alienation was nearly complete . . . at least according to eyewitness accounts of the confirmation ceremony. "None was so sulky and surly as Adolf Hitler," Emmanuel Lugert, a family friend and Hitler's sponsor, later recalled. "I had almost to drag the words out of him. . . . It was almost as though the whole business, the whole confirmation was repugnant to him, as though he only went through it with the greatest reluctance." (What did Hitler do after the ceremony? No kidding—he ran home to play cowboys and Indians with his friends.)

Jesus was crucified, sold at auction for more than $18,000 in May 1993.

SAINTS NO MORE

*Everybody makes mistakes once in a while . . . even the Catholic
Church. Occasionally it declares someone a saint, only to find
out later that the person never existed. Some examples:*

SAINT WILGEFORTIS. One of the most popular saints of
the Middle Ages, Wilgefortis was supposedly the daughter of
a pagan king of Portugal. She was also a devout virgin—and
when her father tried to marry her to the king of Sicily, she prayed
to God to disfigure her so that her suitor would marry someone
else. According to legend she instantly grew a thick moustache
and beard, the sight of which sent the Sicilian packing. (Hence
the name Wilgefortis, a corruption of the words *hilge vartz*—"holy
face".) Her new look made her father so mad that he had her crucified; which is why she is portrayed in art as a bearded woman
nailed to a cross.

Explanation: The saint is the result of a misunderstanding of early
Christian crucifixes, which often portrayed Jesus wearing a long
tunic instead of a loincloth. Medieval Christians misinterpreted
the tunic as a dress, concluded that the wearer (despite the moustache and beard) was a female . . . and invented an entire body of
legends to explain how such a bearded lady came to be crucified.

SAINT PHILOMENA. According to legend, young Philomena
was tortured and murdered after she refused to renounce her virginity and marry the Roman emperor Diocletian.

Background: On May 25, 1802, the skeleton of a fourteen-year-
old girl was discovered in a tomb of one of the Christian catacombs near Rome. Three tiles above the tomb read LVMENA
PAXTE CVM FI—"Lights and peace be with you"—and a small vial
thought to contain traces of blood was found next to the body.
The vial led church authorities to believe that the body was that

The first law commanding clerical celibacy was enacted by the local of a martyr; it was later turned over to a church in Mugnano, Italy, and entombed beneath the altar.

A Saint Is Born: According to Lancelot Sheppard, author of *The Saints Who Never Were*, it was here that the mythmaking began. "An anonymous martyr was not very interesting," he writes, but "the discovery of a martyr with a name was particularly welcomed. The name was obtained, of course, by changing the order of the tiles to make them read PAX TECUM FILVMENA—*'Peace be with you, Philomena.'*" Not long afterwards a priest at the church published an elaborate biography he claimed was inspired by a nun who had had visions of the saint; largely as a result of it, "Saint Philomena" developed a huge following. Her admirers built a shrine in her honor, and in 1855 Pope Pius IX added her feast day to the church's official liturgical calendar.

What Happened: After consulting with archaeologists, in 1961 the Vatican admitted the writing on the tiles had been misinterpreted and that the vial found near the body most likely contained funeral perfumes (common in the catacombs), not the blood of a martyr. That year the church abolished the feast of Philomena, removed her name from the liturgical calendar, and ordered the shrine at Mugnano dismantled.

SAINT EXPEDITUS. Formerly the patron saint of those in urgent need, Saint Expeditus is portrayed in art stomping a black crow that cries *cras* ("tomorrow") while holding aloft a cross with the word *hodie* ("today") written on it—a literalistic depiction of the saying "Never put off until tomorrow what you can do today."

Explanation: According to one version of the story, in the nineteenth century Vatican officials mailed a box of relics to some nuns in Paris. To show when the box had been mailed, the officials wrote the date and the word *spedito* ("sent") on the outside of the box. . . . But when it arrived in Paris, the nuns mistook the word *spedito* to be the name of the saint whose relics were inside. They Latinized it into *Expeditus* and over time created an entire fictional biography around the saint. (Most historians believe the *spedito* story is untrue . . . but they agree the saint never existed.)

SAINT EUSEBIA. According to legend "Saint Eusebia, abbess of a convent at Marseilles, together with her forty companions, cut off their noses to escape outrage by the Saracens," a tribe of Arabian desert nomads. In honor of her sacrifice, Eusebia was interred in a stone coffin that had her likeness carved into the lid . . . complete with a missing nose.

Explanation: When Sister Eusebia died in approximately 680 A.D., her body was laid to rest in a stone coffin that had been carved for someone else—and that had the previous owner's likeness carved into the lid. The coffin was put on display in a cathedral . . . and as the centuries passed the nose wore down to nothing, so much so that later generations assumed the likeness was of a person who had no nose; and someone finally invented a story to go with it. (There is no evidence that Eusebia was considered a saint until *after* the nose on her coffin wore off.)

SAINT NAPOLEON. An Egyptian saint who was allegedly tortured and martyred during the Roman persecutions.

Explanation: Saint Napoleon was actually an eighteenth-century payoff to Emperor Napoleon Bonaparte, who had just signed a concordat with the Vatican and wanted a patron saint in his honor. But there weren't any saints named Napoleon—at least until a French cardinal flipped through the official list of saints, found an obscure one named Neopolus, and renamed it Napoleon. He also wrote a spurious, miracle-filled new biography for the saint and moved its feast day to August 15, Napoleon's birthday.

What Happened: Napoleon Bonaparte fell from power in 1815; his saint followed soon afterwards. It turned out later that even the *original* Saint Neopolus was a fake: Researchers discovered that Neopolus was the name of a *place* in Egypt, not a person, and was mistaken as a saint only through a copyist's error. (Even so, his feast day was still being observed as late as 1960.)

Prince of peace, man of war: Pope John XXIII was a

OUR LADY OF THE 1981 CAMARO

Of the more than 250 reported apparitions of the Virgin Mary between 1928 and 1994, only six have been accepted by the Roman Catholic Church as authentic. Here are some of the ones that didn't make it.

N OW YOU SEE HER . . . *
If you saw an image of the Virgin Mary on the side of your house or in a tree, you'd probably be excited . . . but that's because you aren't a Catholic bishop. "The last thing a bishop wants is for someone to claim the Virgin is coming for a visit," says Father Thomas J. Reese, a Catholic priest and author. "It's a no-win situation. If the bishop says anything against the claim, he is accused of being anti-Mary. And if he encourages it, he may end up looking like a fool."

The church isn't required to investigate the authenticity of reported Mary sightings, but it often does, especially when they begin to draw large crowds. It wants to identify apparitions it believes are truly miraculous (such as Fatima or Lourdes) and expose the ones that are fraudulent or that can be explained by natural phenomena. "In the course of Church history many people have claimed to have had visions," says Denver archbishop J. Francis Stafford, "but the overwhelming majority of cases were not authentic." Some skeptics think *all* the sightings are fake. "Why would a supreme God waste his time appearing in everything from tortillas to bathroom floors?" asks Gerald Larue of the Committee for the Scientific Examination of Religion. "To me this is a very trivial form of divine activity, and it shows how desperate people are to connect to something outside their ordinary lives."

sergeant in the Italian army during World War I.

NOW YOU DON'T . . . (at least according to the Church)

Our Lady of the 1981 Camaro, Brownsville, Texas

The Sighting: In September of 1993, a Texas man looked out his window and saw a crowd of people pointing at the dusty hood of his 1981 Camaro. When he asked what they were doing, they told him the Blessed Virgin had appeared in a dirt stain on the hood.

What Happened: The man washed the car . . . but the image reappeared. So did the crowds. "We've heard the people coming by to see the image won't let the owner move his car," a Brownsville police dispatcher told reporters. The Catholic Church refused to authenticate the apparition, but a spokeswoman told reporters, "If it leads people to prayer, that's good in itself."

Our Lady of the Auto Parts Store, Progreso, Texas

The Sighting: On December 3, 1990, the Virgin Mary appeared in the concrete floor of the Progreso Auto Supply men's room shower . . . at least that's what the store owner says he saw.

What Happened: Within two weeks more than a thousand people a day visited the restroom to weep and pray. Few if any bought auto parts. Some believers took Mary's unfortunate location—on the floor of an auto parts store shower—personally. "I feel guilty," one distraught woman declared. "I'm part to blame for where she is."

Our Lady of Baza, Spain

Background: In 1993 Sanchez Casas, an eighteen-year-old Spanish faith healer, announced that on June 11 the Virgin Mary would appear to any of his followers who "looked directly at the sun."

What Happened: On June 11, an estimated one thousand of his followers travelled to Baza, looked directly at the sun . . . and suffered severe eye damage. More than thirty people were hospitalized, and at least eight suffered permanent vision loss. (Casas

The Vatican has its own supermarket, train station, jail, pharmacy, post office . . .

pooh-poohed the stricken as "nonbelievers" who had "stared at the sun on the wrong day.")

Our Lady of Denver, Colorado
Background: In November 1991 a Denver woman announced to the world that the Blessed Virgin would appear at a Catholic shrine on Assumption Day—and that "great favors" would be rained upon those who witnessed the holy event. (How did the woman know? She claimed that Mary had told her so in a vision.)
What Happened: More than six thousand people—many of them elderly and infirm—traveled to the shrine in below-freezing temperatures to witness the "miracle" and spent the entire day staring into the sky waiting for something to happen. Nothing did . . . but as in Baza, some of the pilgrims looked directly at the sun. At least two dozen people suffered permanent loss of vision; others suffered permanent loss of faith. "Did you ever hear of people going to Jesus for a miracle," one partially blinded woman asked, "and coming away crippled?"

Our Lady of the Backyard, Marlboro, New Jersey
The Sighting: In 1992 Marlboro citizen Joseph Januszkiewicz told the world that the Virgin Mary had appeared to him in his backyard on the first Sunday of each month and would keep doing so.
What Happened: The monthly visits attracted as many as ten thousand of the faithful to Marlboro (population 28,000)— costing the town as much as $21,000 in police patrols and "sanitation overtime" per visit. On September 25, 1992, the health department ordered Januszkiewicz to install ten portable toilets on his property to meet his pilgrims' nonspiritual needs. Health officials took the action after receiving "vivid accounts of people defecating in the woods and bushes."

Our Lady of Cold Spring, Kentucky
Background: In August 1992, Reverend LeRoy Smith of Saint

and its own parish church, St. Anne of the Palafrenieri.

Joseph Catholic Church in Cold Spring told his congregation that a visionary had predicted that the Virgin Mary would make an appearance at the church at midnight on September 1. He never identified the visionary.

What Happened: Six thousand people showed up to see if Mary would appear. Whether or not she did depends on who you ask: Some people saw her on the side of the church; others saw her in a nearby tree. One woman saw lights outside the church that she was sure *represented* the Blessed Virgin. But most people didn't see anything, including William Hughes, the local bishop. "I am convinced that nothing of a miraculous nature occurred," he reported the next day. Still, Ms. Dang and others haven't changed their minds. "The bishop is a mortal man," she said later, "and he could make a mistake."

. . . LAST BUT NOT LEAST

Our Lady of Medjugorje. In June 1981, two teenagers were sneaking cigarettes on the side of a hill overlooking Medjugorje in Bosnia-Herzegovina when the Virgin Mary appeared to them in the clouds. Four other teenagers made similar sightings not long afterwards (no word on what they were smoking), and the story spread round the world. Since then more than 15 million of the faithful have made pilgrimages to the site.

What Happened: Despite Medjugorje's immense popularity with pilgrims (before the Bosnian civil war it drew almost as many people as Fatima and Lourdes), so far the church says the sightings are bunk. The Vatican officially discourages pilgrims from going there, and the local bishop has denounced the sightings as "collective hallucinations" that some Franciscan priests are exploiting in an attempt to gain control of a local parish. In a 1991 statement, nineteen of twenty Yugoslav bishops declared that "on the basis of research conducted so far, one cannot affirm that supernatural apparitions are involved."

One major reason for the skepticism: Theologians say the

many messages supposedly delivered by Mary are too similar—and boring—to be authentic. "All the messages I've seen from Medjugorje can be reduced to one word, conversion," says Father Giandomenico Mucci. "One does not understand why Mary must repeat herself like that. Nor can one understand the banality of the language."

The Aftermath: The pilgrims keep on coming, even as civil war rages . . . and a cottage industry of pizza parlors, hot dog stands, and foreign exchange booths has sprung up to serve them. "The atmosphere is like Mary World," one Florida-based pilgrim told reporters. "I spent most of my time buying rosaries." Even the outbreak of bloody civil war hasn't stopped visitors entirely. "I've had open-heart surgery, a ruptured appendix, a gall bladder removed, a back operation, a plugged carotid artery, an angioplasty, and I'm on my second pacemaker," another pilgrim told *The Wall Street Journal* while a fierce battle raged just outside of town. "You think I'm afraid of a little shooting?"

✠   ✠   ✠

. . . YOU'VE GOT TO HAND IT TO THESE SAINTS

Saint Nicholas of Tolentino (1245-1305). About a year after Saint Nicholas died in 1305, a German friar cut the arms off of his corpse to take them back to Germany. The friar walked all night with the arms, but when the sun came up the next morning he realized he had not moved from the place where he had started. He returned the arms, and they were eventually reattached to the corpse. According to legend, the arms bleed whenever the city is in danger.

Saint John Damascene (675-749), who is portrayed in art holding his severed right hand in his left hand. Why? According to legend a Muslim potentate chopped off his hand and nailed it to the city gate . . . but the Virgin Mary appeared and reattached it. (He died intact at the age of seventy-four.)

MORE CATHOLIC
WORD ORIGINS

*Another collection of everyday words you probably
had no idea were inspired by the Catholic Church.*

BEDLAM

Meaning: Craziness or confusion.

Background: The Catholic Church founded London's Saint Mary
of Bethlehem monastery (pronounced *bedlam* by the locals) in
1247. King Henry VIII seized it in the sixteenth century and converted into an insane asylum; but he left the name unchanged. In
time the asylum's reputation as a madhouse grew so notorious that
the word "bedlam" became synonymous for madness or confusion.

GARDEN

Meaning: A place set aside for growing fruits and vegetables.

Background: The Romans introduced horticulture to England in
the first century A.D.—but when they abandoned the island in the
fifth century, gardening died out except among monasteries and
other religious institutions, whose gardens and orchards were often
surrounded by walls or fences to *guard* against cattle and wild animals. These protected spaces became known as *guardins*, a name
that eventually came to describe any planted plot of land . . .
whether or not it was guarded.

IN HOCK

Meaning: In debt.

Background: Hocktide was a weeklong festival celebrated in
England during the twelfth century. On Monday the women of a
village ambushed the men, tied them up, and refused to let them
go until they made a ransom payment of some kind. On Tuesday

the men did the same thing to the women; afterwards the ransom money from both days was donated to the church. Over time anyone who owed money was said to be "in Hocktide"—an expression that was later shortened to "in hock."

RAISING CAIN

Meaning: Causing trouble.

Background: The eighteenth century was an age in which children were supposed to be seen and not heard. Parents who raised rowdy, undisciplined children were said to be *raising Cains*: children who would grow up to be like the biblical Cain (who murdered his brother Abel and then denied responsibility when questioned by God). Over time, "raising cain" came to refer the *act* of unruliness, not the child-rearing itself.

TAWDRY

Meaning: Cheap or shoddy.

Background: Saint Audrey was an abbess on the English Island of Ely during the seventh century. She died of a breast tumor in 679, which she blamed on the expensive jeweled necklaces she wore as a child. For centuries the citizens of Ely held an annual Saint Audrey festival and women wore lace necklaces—nicknamed "Taudry's lace" after the saint's nickname—to mark the event. The original necklaces were quite ornate, but they spawned an entire cottage industry of cheap imitation lace, whose quality was so poor that the name "taudry" came to symbolize shoddiness.

X

Meaning: The kiss symbol used at the end of letters.

Background: In the Middle Ages, illiterate peasants who couldn't sign their names on important documents wrote an X instead—the mark of Saint Andrew. On *really* important documents the peasant had to kiss the X as a further sign of his sincerity. By the twentieth century the X and its kiss were completely synonymous.

Top 4 religions in the U.S.: Protestantism, Catholicism, Judaism, and . . . Buddhism.

THE NAME'S FAMILIAR. . .

You've heard of Saint Bernard dogs, Saint Elmo's Fire, and Saint Patrick's Day . . . But do you know anything about the saints they're named after? Here's a crash course on who they were.

SAINT PATRICK (c. 390-c. 461). The son of a Scottish deacon, Saint Patrick was captured by pirates at the age of sixteen, taken to Ireland, and forced to work as a shepherd. Six years later he returned to Scotland and became a priest. He eventually returned to Ireland, converted it to Christianity, and according to legend rid it of snakes. (He's also credited with driving the ants out of Puerto Rico, but they came back.) It was his legendary use of the shamrock to explain how the Father, the Son, and the Holy Spirit are all the one God that made the symbol synonymous with Saint Patrick's Day.

SAINT ELMO (c. 250-300). The inspiration for Saint Elmo's Fire, the lighteninglike static electricity that often discharges on ships at sea. Not much is known of Saint Elmo, but according to legend he was preaching a sermon one day when lightening suddenly struck the ground beside him. He amazed onlookers by continuing to preach as if nothing had happened; not long afterwards sailors began invoking his name against thunderstorms at sea. They interpreted the static electricity that discharged harmlessly on their boats as a sign that their prayers had been answered.

SAINT VINCENT DE PAUL (1581-1660). In his lifetime Saint Vincent, a French priest, founded twenty-five charity houses, several hospitals, and cofounded the Institute of the Sisters of Charity, the first women's religious order dedicated to helping the poor and sick. He also worked with prisoners and war victims and sent missionaries all over Europe. The Society of Saint Vincent de Paul, an association of Catholic laypeople devoted to serving the poor, was founded in his honor in 1833.

Pope Pius XII (1939-1958) had a papal throne in his elevator at the Vatican Palace.

SAINT ANTHONY OF PADUA (1195-1231). Saint Anthony is the guy that generations of Catholics have prayed to for help in finding lost items. Why? According to legend, when a young friar stole a book from a monastery that Anthony had founded, he was confronted by a fearful apparition that told him to take it back. (He did.)

SAINT BERNARD (c. 996-1081). Bernard of Montjoux was an Italian priest who built rest houses for religious pilgrims at the tops of two mountain passes in the European Alps . . . but he had nothing to do with the dogs that bear his name—his successors didn't develop the breed until centuries after his death.

SAINT JOAN OF ARC (1412-1431). The pious daughter of a peasant farmer, Joan of Arc began having supernatural visions of Saint Michael, Saint Catherine, Saint Margaret, and other saints, at the age of 13. Her mission in life, she claimed they told her, was to save France from defeat in the Hundred Years' War, then in its eighty-ninth year, by helping the dauphin Charles of France (son of the mad King Charles VI of France) become king in his own right. After convincing him to let her lead his armies into bat-tle—which wasn't easy, considering she was only seventeen at the time—she raised the siege of Orléans and won a major victory against the British on June 18, 1429. She attacked Paris a few months later, but failed to liberate it, and was captured in May 1430. She was burned at the stake a year later.
Note: Joan of Arc was virtually unknown before the nineteenth century and didn't become a saint until 1920. (Technically speak-ing, she wasn't even a citizen of France— she was born in 1412 in Domrémy, which at that time was independent from France.) But Napoleon Bonaparte needed a legendary figure that he could use to inspire French nationalism, and Joan of Arc was just the woman for the job.

Famous forgotten Catholic: James Hoban, who designed the White House in 1792.

HOLY HELPERS

Got a problem big or small? A saint's the one you need to call!
Here are some more saints and their specialties:

Sore Eyes: St. Clare (also the patroness of television)

Oversleeping: St. Vitus

Communists: St. Joseph

Protection from Fools, Clowns and Idiots: St. Mathurin

Nightmares: St. Christopher

Invoked against Flies (and Their Maggots): St. Leufredus

Invoked against Other Insects: St. Dominic of Silos

Protection *from* Freethinkers: St. Titus

Protection from Perjurers: St. Felix of Nola

Stuttering: St. Notker the Stammerer

Stiff Backs and Necks: St. Albert of Trapani

Vampires: St. Marcel of Paris

Juvenile Delinquents: St. Dominic Savio

Invoked against Whirlpools: St. Goar

Travellers Seeking Good Lodging: St. Julian

Gambling Addiction: St. Bernardino of Siena

Demonic Possession: St. Bruno

Backward Children: St. Hilary of Poitiers

Illegitimate Children: St. John Francis Regis

Children "Who Are Late in Learning to Walk": St. Vaast

Sick Chickens: St. Ferreolus

Servants "Who Break Things": St. Benedict

Leg Diseases: St. Servatus

"Those Who are Insane": St. Véran

Jesus had 12 apostles and 72 disciples at the time of his death.

CATHOLIC QUIZ #3
AT THE MOVIES

When you consider that the Catholic Church is the largest religion in the U.S., it's not surprising that a lot of movies over the years have been made with Roman Catholics in mind. See if you can answer the following film questions. Answers are on page 199.

1. Originally titled *The Padre*, this Catholic classic languished in the Paramount Studios film vault for more than six months because studio executives feared the Catholic Church would find it offensive. What film was it?

    (A) *The Name of the Rose* (1986), starring Sean Connery as a fourteenth-century monk.

    (B) *Boys' Town* (1938), Spencer Tracy stars as Father Flanagan, the founder of Boys' Town, a home for abused handicapped children in Nebraska.

    (C) *Going My Way* (1944), starring Bing Crosby as Father Chuck O'Malley, a singing priest.

2. In the 1943 film *The Song of Bernadette*, twenty-four-year-old Jennifer Jones plays Saint Bernadette Soubirous, the young girl who had a vision of the Virgin Mary at Lourdes. It was Jones's first major film role, but her performance was so stunning that she beat out Ingrid Bergman to win the Oscar for Best Actress. Even so, casting her for the part generated controversy behind the scenes. Why?

    (A) Jones, who plays a girl who becomes a nun (and later a saint), was a married woman with two children . . . and was on the verge of divorcing her husband when the film premiered.

    (B) Jones was a devout Lutheran—and the Catholic Church frowned on casting non-Catholics as saints.

"Man was made to rule, woman to obey." —Saint Augustine (354-430)

(C) Jones looked pretty holy on film, but she had been kicked out of two Carmelite boarding schools and a women's college run by the Sisters of Charity . . . and the nuns from her old schools mounted a nationwide letter-writing campaign to get her kicked off the film.

3. What biblical-period epic is the only movie based on a novel that has been blessed by a pope?
    (A) *The Ten Commandments* (1956)
    (B) *Ben Hur* (1959)
    (C) *Samson and Delilah* (1949)

4. Who played a nun opposite Elvis Presley in the 1969 film *Change of Habit?*
    (A) Angie Dickinson
    (B) Meryl Streep
    (C) Mary Tyler Moore

5. What film changed its name after the original title was deemed too offensive for contemporary religious standards?
    (A) *Monty Python's Life of Brian* (1979)
    (B) *The Pope Must Die* (1991)
    (C) *The Last Temptation of Christ* (1988)

6. Which unlikely star was cast as a Roman Catholic priest in the 1948 film *The Miracle of the Bells?*
    (A) Frank Sinatra
    (B) Humphrey Bogart
    (C) Groucho Marx

7. What film based on a Pulitzer Prize-winning play almost never made it onto the screen thanks to opposition from the Catholic Church . . . but went on to win four Oscars?

The Vatican has its own heliport . . . but it doesn't own a helicopter.

(A) *Death of a Salesman* (1985)
(B) *A Streetcar Named Desire* (1951)
(C) *To Kill a Mockingbird* (1962)

8. What actress, after she learned of her nomination for Best Supporting Actress for her role as a nun, replied, "It means a lot to me, but next year it's going to be a Trivial Pursuit question."
(A) Debra Winger
(B) Jodie Foster
(C) Meg Tilly

✛   ✛   ✛

. . . TWO THUMBS DOWN
More movie reviews from the National Catholic Film Office:

The Last Picture Show (1971)
"There seem to be no normal, much less wholesome or happy sexual relationships [in the film]. . . . Everyone commits acts of adultery, fornication, and perversion slavishly and joylessly. . . . One might compare their impersonal sexual frenzy to that of spawning salmon, but salmon, at least, act according to nature and to propagate their kind."

American Gigolo (1978)
". . . There is much nudity and graphic sexuality, and the moral stance is quite muddled."

All That Jazz (1980)
"A workaholic, womanizing Broadway director-choreographer (he is also a hotshot film director, this whiz) drives himself, quite literally, to death while rehearsing a new musical....The exuberant celebration of the hero's moral failings, the nihilistic mood and some grossly lewd dance sequences are extremely offensive."

(That is supplied by the Italian military.)

CHAPTER AND VERSE

*Have you read your Bible lately? Let's face it—most of us
haven't read it in a long time. . . . Here are some of the
more unusual passages we've been missing.*

MIXED MESSAGES
"And Jesus told this parable: 'A man had a fig tree planted in his
vineyard; and he came seeking fruit on it and found none. And he
said to the vinedresser, "Lo, these three years I have come seeking
fruit on this fig tree, and I found none. Cut it down; why should it
use up the ground?" And he answered him, "Let it alone, sir, this
year also, till I dig about it and put on manure. And if it bears fruit
next year, well and good; but if not, you can cut it down."' "
—Luke 13:6-9

"In the morning, as [Jesus] was returning to the city, he was hungry. And seeing a fig tree by the wayside he went to it, and found
nothing on it but leaves only. And he said to it, 'May no fruit ever
come from you again!' And the fig tree withered at once."
—Matthew 21:18-19

FAMILY VALUES
"Now great multitudes accompanied [Jesus]; and he turned and
said to them, 'If any one comes to me and does not hate his own
father and mother and wife and children and brothers and sisters,
yes, and even his own life, he cannot be my disciple.' "
—Luke 14:25-26

To his disciples: "Do not think that I have come to bring peace on
earth; I have not come to bring peace, but a sword. For I have
come to set a man against his father, and a daughter against her
mother, and a daughter-in-law against her mother-in-law; and a
man's foes will be those of his own household. He who loves

father or mother more than me is not worthy of me; and he who does not take his cross and follow me is not worthy of me. He who finds his life will lose it, and he who loses his life for my sake will find it."

—Matthew 10:34-39

DUST TO DUST
"And [Jesus] called to him the twelve [apostles], and began to send them out two by two, and gave them authority over the unclean spirits. . . . And he said to them, 'Where you enter a house, stay there until you leave the place. And if any place will not receive you and they refuse to hear you, when you leave, shake off the dust that is on your feet for a testimony against them.' "

—Mark 6:7-11

JESUS INSPIRES THE TELEVANGELISTS
"Now when Jesus was at Bethany in the house of Simon the leper, a woman came up to him with an alabaster flask of very expensive ointment, and she poured it on his head, as he sat at table. But when the disciples saw it, they were indignant, saying, 'Why this waste? For this ointment might have been sold for a large sum, and given to the poor.' But Jesus, aware of this, said to them, 'Why do you trouble the woman? For she has done a beautiful thing to me. For you always have the poor with you, but you will not always have me.' "

—Matthew 26:6-11

SALTY LANGUAGE
To John the Apostle: "Salt is good, but if the salt has lost its saltiness, how will you season it? Have salt in yourselves, and be at peace with one another.' "

—Mark 9:50

Canon law allows popes to resign if they want to. (Few do.)

PILLARS OF VIRTUE

How does a person achieve holiness? And if, like Mother Teresa,
you do achieve it, how do you keep religious groupies from following
you around all the time? Some of the early saints managed to answer
both questions at once—they literally put themselves on a pedestal.

TALL TALES

Fleeing the evils of the world to contemplate God alone in silence and prayer is one of the oldest traditions of the Catholic Church. It developed in the third and fourth centuries, when the first hermits and ascetics fled into the wilderness as the anti-Christian persecutions of the Roman Empire waned and post-persecution Christian lifestyles became too soft. Most hermits led pretty unremarkable lives: They lived in caves or small shelters devoid of material pleasures, eating food that they gathered or that was brought to them by admirers. But over time some of them turned to more severe forms of self-denial, including sleep deprivation, exposure to the elements, and extreme fasting that approached starvation. Some of the sacrifices they made were just plain weird—so much so that the early saints made note of them in their writings, as the *Catholic Encyclopedia* recounted in 1902:

> St. Palladius tells us of a hermit in Palestine who dwelt in a cave on the top of a mountain and who for the space of twenty-five years never turned his face to the West. St. Gregory of Nazianzus speaks of a solitary who stood upright for many years . . . absorbed in contemplation, without ever lying down. Theodoret assures us that he had seen a hermit who had passed ten years in a tub suspended in midair from poles. . . . [Such accounts] must pass belief, but the evidence is overwhelming and the correctness of the accounts preserved to us is now hardly disputed.

Taking the High Ground

But perhaps the most bizarre form of asceticism was that of the fifth-century *stylites* or pillar saints, men (and a few women) who lived out their lives on tall columns not more than a few feet wide and who, in many cases, never came down—not even to eat, sleep or go, to the bathroom. How did they survive? Most were fed by the scores of followers they attracted. (No word on how they went to the bathroom, but it is assumed that similar arrangements were made . . . or that admirers kept their distance.)

A TOWERING PERSONALITY
Worshipping Christ by living on a pole was apparently the brainchild of Saint Simeon Stylite the Elder (388-459), the man historians regard as the father of the stylite movement. Eccentric even in his youth, Simeon joined a monastery at the age of sixteen but was kicked out after practicing austerities "so extreme and to all appearances so extravagant, that his brethren judged him, perhaps not unwisely, to be unsuited to any form of community life."

For the next several years Simeon practiced increasingly harsh forms of self-denial. He lived in an abandoned water tank for three years; then he graduated to "standing continually upright so long as his limbs would sustain him." When that didn't prove severe enough, he moved to an outcropping of rock in the desert and confined himself within a narrow space less than twenty yards in diameter.

Pole Position
The only problem: As Simeon grew weirder he began to draw crowds, as mobs of the faithful (and not a few gawkers) started seeking him out for spiritual aid and advice. He had almost no time for himself—and it was at this point that, in the words of one wag, "despairing of escaping the world horizontally, he tried to escape it vertically." In 423 A.D. he built a ten-foot-high column out of three large stones (representing the Trinity) and perched himself atop it, vowing never to come down. Though the living surface was only six feet in diameter and offered no shelter from the elements, he lived there continuously for the next thirty-six years, adding stones over time until the column was more than sixty feet tall.

ceremony in Seoul, South Korea—the largest mass canonization in church history.

Life at the top was no picnic—according to one account, "Simeon practiced the greatest austerities, slept little if at all, was clad only in the skins of wild beasts, and fasted completely during Lent for 40 years." Though he was annoyed by the crowds that gathered below, Simeon remained as accessible to them as one can be on top of a sixty-foot pillar, as the *Catholic Encyclopedia* describes:

> By means of a ladder which could always be erected against the side, visitors were able to ascend. . . . He wrote letters, he instructed disciples, and he also delivered addresses to those assembled beneath. . . . Great personages, such as the Emperor and Empress, manifested the utmost reverence for this saint and listened to his councils.

OTHER CATHOLIC COLUMNISTS

Saint Simeon Stylite the Elder died on September 2, 459, but not before inspiring a host of imitators and innovators, among them:

Saint Simeon Stylite the Younger (517–592). One of the youngest of the stylites. A disciple of a man named Saint John Stylite, Simeon moved onto his first pillar at the age of seven and continued the lifestyle for the next sixty-eight years. "In the course of this time," notes the *Catholic Encyclopedia*, "he several times moved to a new pillar, and on the occasion of the first of these exchanges was ordained a deacon during the short space of time he spent on the ground." He attracted followers who erected their own pillars; together they formed a small but dedicated pillar community, whose columns were far enough apart to afford some measure of privacy but close enough that they could speak to one another without shouting.

At the age of thirty Simeon had a vision (which isn't surprising, considering his lifestyle) that told him to found a monastery. So he did; it too consisted largely of pillars. Three years later he was ordained a priest, and for the rest of his life he celebrated Mass

Famous forgotten date: November 18, 1966, the last meatless Friday.

from the top of the pillar, where crowds of people climbed ladders to receive communion from his hands.

Saint Simeon Stylite III. According to the *Catholic Encyclopedia*, "It must be confessed that very little certain is known of him. He is believed to have been struck by lightning upon his pillar."

Saint Alypius. "After standing upright for fifty-three years, he found his feet no longer able to support him; but instead of descending from his pillar, he lay down on his side and spent the remaining fourteen years of his life in that position."

Saint Daniel Stylite. Not quite as austere as some of the other stylites, Saint Daniel lived on top of *two* pillars connected by a wooden walkway with railings. According to one source, "hereon he was ordained priest and celebrated the Eucharist, and came down only once in thirty-three years, to reprove an erring emperor." He died at age eighty-nine and was buried at the base of his pillar. (No word on *which* pillar. . . .)

The Hollow-Pillar Hermits. A small group of nonconformists who built hollow pillars and lived *inside* of them instead of upon them, which offered slightly more protection from the elements.

✠　　✠　　✠

POPE-PROGANDA

In 1622 Pope Gregory XV established the *Congregatio de Propaganda Fide*, a committee of cardinals assigned the task of establishing missions in foreign lands in order to "propagate" or spread the faith. The *faith* didn't become universal, but the *word* "propaganda"—information designed to win a person over to a particular point of view—did: By the nineteenth century it referred to information used to spread *any* set of beliefs . . . even if they weren't Catholic.

The Sistine Chapel is named after Pope Sixtus IV, the pope who ordered it built.

STRANGERS IN THE NIGHT

*Does the name "Father Casanova" sound odd to you? Then you may be
surprised to learn that Giovanni Casanova, history's best-known
seducer, actually spent time in a seminary studying for the
priesthood. You'll never guess why he got kicked out . . .*

C ARNAL KNOWLEDGE
In 1789 Giovanni Jacopo Casanova published *The Story of
My Life*, a twelve-volume, 4,545-page autobiography that
described in lurid detail his sexual encounters with more than 130
women, including opera singers, noblewomen, at least one nun (he
kept a lock of her pubic hair as a momento), and the wife of the
mayor of Cologne. *The Story of My Life* reads like something out of
Penthouse magazine: It starts off by describing eleven-year-old Giovanni's sexual awakening at the hands of his landlord's sister, who
massaged him into arousal while giving him a bath; afterwards it
relates how he lost his virginity to two sisters, Nanette and Marton
Savorgnan, when he was seventeen.

After that the story *really* gets interesting, at least from a
Catholic perspective: When Giovanni's mother learned of the
ménage à trois, she tried to break it up by enrolling him in a seminary. "The plan . . . was absurd," Casanova admits in his autobiography, "for at the age of seventeen, and with a nature like mine,
the idea of placing me in a seminary ought never to have been
entertained." Within a month he was caught in bed with one of
the other students and expelled. In his memoirs Casanova denies
that anything illicit took place (although he does admit to having
a number of homosexual affairs later in life) and claims that the
incident that got him expelled was a case of mistaken identity.
Either way, the story makes for great reading. Here it is in his own
words:

Eighty-eight percent of U.S. nuns say that if they could start

AT THE SEMINARY
"I entered the seminary at the beginning of March, and prepared myself for my new life by passing the night between my two young friends, Nanette and Marton. . . . Any lover who knows what his feelings were when he found himself with the woman he adored and with the fear that it was for the last time, will easily imagine my feelings during the last hours that I expected ever to spend with my two charming mistresses. I could not be induced to let the last offering be the last, and I went on offering until there was no more incense left. . . .

"One of [my dormitory companions], about fifteen years old, and who at the present time must, if still alive, be a bishop, attracted my notice by his features as much as by his talents. He inspired me with a very warm friendship, and during recess, instead of playing skittles with the others, we always walked together. . . . We were such fast friends, after four days of acquaintance, that we were actually jealous of each other, and to such an extent that if either of us walked about with any seminarist, the other would be angry and sulk like a disappointed lover."

HOUSE RULES
"The dormitory was placed under the supervision of a lay friar, and it was his province to keep us in good order. After supper, accompanied by this lay friar, who had the title of prefect, we all proceeded to the dormitory. There, everyone had to go to his own bed, and to undress quietly after having said his prayers in a low voice. When all the pupils were in bed, the prefect would go to his own. A large lantern lighted up the dormitory, which had the shape of a parallelogram eighty yards by ten. The beds were placed at equal distances, and to each bed there were a fald-stool, a chair, and room for the trunk of the Seminarist. At one end was the washing place, and at the other the bed of the prefect. The bed of my friend was opposite mine, and the lantern was between us. . . .

their lives over, they'd become nuns all over again.

"The principal duty of the prefect was to take care that no pupil should go and sleep with one of his comrades, for such a visit was never supposed an innocent one. It was a cardinal sin, and, bed being accounted the place for sleep and not for conversation, it was admitted that a pupil who slept out of his own bed, did so only for immoral purposes. So long as he stopped in his own bed, he could do what he liked; so much the worse for him if he gave himself up to bad practices. . . . "

THE FIRST ENCOUNTER

"I had been in the seminary for nine or ten days, when one night I felt someone stealing very quietly in my bed; my hand was at once clutched, and my name whispered. I could hardly restrain my laughter. It was my friend, who, having chanced to wake up and finding that the lantern was out, had taken a sudden fancy to pay me a visit. I very soon begged him to go away for fear the prefect should be awake, for in such a case we should have found ourselves in a very unpleasant dilemma, and most likely would have been accused of some abominable offense. As I was giving him that good advice we heard someone moving, and my friend made his escape; but immediately after he had left me I heard the fall of some person, and at the same time the hoarse voice of the prefect exclaiming: 'Ah, villain ! wait until tomorrow—until tomorrow !' After which threat he lighted the lantern and retired to his couch."

CONFRONTATION

"The next morning, before the ringing of the bell for rising, the rector, followed by the prefect, entered the dormitory, and said to us: 'Listen to me, all of you. You are aware of what has taken place this last night. Two amongst you must be guilty; but I wish to forgive them, and to save their honor I promise that their names shall not be made public. I expect every one of you to come to me for confession before recess.'

"He left the dormitory, and we dressed ourselves. In the afternoon, in obedience to his orders, we all went to him and confessed, after which ceremony we repaired to the garden, where my friend told me that, having unfortunately met the prefect after he left me, he had thought that the best way was to knock him down, in order to get time to reach his own bed without being known."

True Confessions
" ' And now,' I said, 'you are certain of being forgiven, for, of course, you have wisely confessed your error?' 'You are joking,' answered my friend; 'why, the good rector would not have known any more than he knows at present, even if my visit to you had been paid with a criminal intent.'

" 'Then you must have made a false confession: you are at all events guilty of disobedience?'

" 'That may be, but the rector is responsible for the guilt, as he used compulsion.'

" 'My dear friend, you argue in a very forcible way, and the very reverend rector must by this time be satisfied that the inmates of our dormitory are more learned than he is himself.' "

THE SECOND ENCOUNTER
"No more would have been said about the adventure if, a few nights after, I had not in my turn taken a fancy to return the visit paid by my friend. Towards midnight, having had occasion to get out of bed, and hearing the loud snoring of the prefect, I quickly put out the lantern and went to lie beside my friend. He knew me at once, and gladly received me; but we both listened attentively to the snoring of our keeper, and when it ceased, understanding our danger, I got up and reached my own bed without losing a second, but the moment I got to it I had a double surprise.

"In the first place I felt somebody lying in my bed, and in the second I saw the prefect, with a candle in his hand, coming along slowly and taking a survey of all the beds right and left. I

Karol Wojtyla, 3 days before he was elected Pope John Paul II.

could understand the prefect suddenly lighting a candle, but how could I realize what I saw—namely, one of my comrades sleeping soundly in my bed, with his back turned to me?"

Quick Thinking
"I immediately made up my mind to feign sleep. After two or three shakings given by the prefect, I pretended to wake up, and my bed-companion woke up in earnest. Astonished at finding himself in my bed, he offered me an apology: 'I have made a mistake,' he said, 'as I returned from a certain place in the dark, I found your bed empty, and mistook it for mine.'

" 'Very likely,' I answered; 'I had to get up, too.'

" 'Yes,' remarked the prefect; 'but how does it happen that you went to bed without making any remark when, on your return, you found your bed already tenanted? And how is it that, being in the dark, you did not suppose that you were mistaken yourself?'

" 'I could not be mistaken, for I felt the pedestal of this crucifix of mine, and I knew I was right; as to my companion here, I did not feel him.'

" 'It is all very unlikely,' answered our Argus; and he went to the lantern, the wick of which he found crushed down.

" 'The wick has been forced into the oil, gentlemen; it has not gone out of itself; it has been the handiwork of one of you, but it will be seen to in the morning.' "

WHAT HAPPENED
The next morning Casanova and the other boy were hauled before the rector and the prefect to account for their behavior. Both boys were beaten with sticks, locked in separate cells for four days, and then expelled. Casanova returned to his girlfriends and, as he put it, "quickly made up for lost time." He went on to live a full life, to say the least. But his profligate ways eventually caught up with him: In addition to bouts with smallpox, pleurisy, pneumonia, and

Priest shortage: An estimated 600 counties in the U.S. have no Catholic priests at all.

two cases of malaria, he contracted syphilis and gonorrhea at least eleven times by the age of forty. This, combined with the toxic mercury therapy used to treat venereal disease in those days, left him completely impotent by the age of sixty. Deprived of sex, he turned to food with a vengeance. In the words of one biographer, "since he could no longer be a god in the gardens, he became a wolf at the table." He died of kidney failure and an inflamed prostate in 1798. He was seventy-three.

RECOMMENDED READING
The Memoirs of Jacques Casanova de Seingalt, translated by Arthur Machen (1894). (*Check your bookstore or public library for the latest reissue.*)

✠ ✠ ✠

. . . BOB GUCCIONE, EX-SEMINARIAN
Here's another unlikely candidate for the priesthood who actually spent time in a seminary: Bob Guccione, the publisher of Penthouse *magazine. Peter Occiogrosso interviewed him for his book* Once a Catholic:
"I went to Sunday school for a number of years while I was growing up. But I think that by the time I was twelve or thirteen I started to drift away from the Church. . . . Just prior to quitting the church physically—I didn't ever quit it emotionally or even psychically—I got so interested that I even wanted to become a priest. . . . I was very devout, very much caught up in the religion, and I went to a seminary for a while. I liked it. I was pretty dedicated. . . . One thing I learned and maintain to this day . . . is that I developed a great respect for women."

The pope has his own passport: Vatican City passport #1.

JUNK MAIL FOR JESUS

You can't help but end up on a lot of unusual mailing lists when you write a book about the Catholic Church. Here's one of the strangest letters I've gotten to date. It's from Father Bob at the Sacred Heart Auto League.

Dear Friend,
We see it more often than we would like . . . two cars crushed together in the middle of an intersection, an ugly confusion of twisted metal, broken glass, and spilled antifreeze. Police cars, tow trucks, and ambulances add more anxiety to the disturbing scene. . . . More than 50,000 motorists are killed in traffic accidents each year! And 200,000 more suffer painful injuries, or permanent disabilities.

Careless and reckless drivers cause most traffic accidents. We all know the type: people who ignore the rules of the road, people who lack common courtesy, people who drive at excessive speeds, those who drink and drive.

When the picture looks so frightening you may wonder to yourself: "But what can I do about traffic accidents? I don't do those things. The situation is out of my control."

That is not true! You don't have to feel helpless. You can chose to take positive action as have thousands and thousands of drivers across the country.

You can become a member of the Sacred Heart Auto League and devote your driving and travel time to the Sacred Heart.

. . . The Sacred Heart Auto League is not a gimmick.
Nor does membership give you some magic power to avoid all accidents. But it does make driving a prayerful and serious business.

It provides you with the graces of a Holy Mass offered daily for Auto League members. It can give you a sense of power over what is often a frustrating or sometimes frightening task—driving.

Poll result: 59% of Catholic priests think the church should ordain married men . . .

And like hundreds of thousands of other members, you can feel proud to belong to a group of committed Catholics who see the value of dedicating a routine but important task to the Glory of God. I invite you to join today. There are no membership fees. Any gift you send will be used to help spread devotion to the Sacred Heart through the League's many apostolic works.

Membership is as easy as one, two, three. . .

1) Pledge to become a prayerful, careful driver.

2) Sign your membership card and pray the Driver's Prayer each time you travel in a motor vehicle:

> God our Father, you led Abraham from his home and guard-
> ed him in all his wanderings. You guided him safely to the
> destination you had chosen for him. Be with us now as we
> travel. Be our safety every mile of the way. Make us atten-
> tive, cautious, and concerned about our fellow travelers.
> Make our highways safe and keep us from all danger. Guide
> us to our destination for today and may it bring us one day
> closer to our final destination with you. We pray this in
> Jesus' name. Amen.

3) Complete the enclosed Membership Enrollment Form and return it to me in the envelope provided.

Attach the attractive new Sacred Heart Auto League Emblem to the dashboard of your car. . . . Each time you travel in your auto-mobile the image of the Sacred Heart will remind you of your pledge of safe driving. And you will know that you and your trav-eling companions are under His protection. . . .

May the Sacred Heart protect and bless you every mile you travel.

> Sincerely in the Sacred Heart,
> Father Bob Hess
> President and Spiritual Director

FOR MORE INFORMATION

Want to hear more? Contact Father Bob Hess at Sacred Heart Auto League, Walls, Mississippi 38686-0201.

but only 15% said they would marry if permitted to do so.

THE INNOCENTS

*Today's popes choose fairly common names when they're elected pope
(John, Paul, John Paul, etc.)—but the pontiffs of old were much more
creative. Take for example, the thirteen popes (and one anti-pope) who
chose the name "Innocent." Not all of them lived up to the title . . .*

I **nnocent II (1130-1143).** Helped rig his own papal election:
The College of Cardinals was split between conservatives and
reformers when Pope Honorius II died on the night of February
14, 1130—and rather than risk losing a fair election, the reformers
proclaimed Innocent II pope at sunrise . . . without even telling
the conservatives that Honorius had died. They found out three
hours later and elected their own pope, Anacletus II, igniting an
eight-year power struggle that didn't end until Anacletus died in
1138 . . . and Innocent finally bribed enough conservatives into
making him the undisputed head of the Catholic Church.

Innocent III (1198-1216). Probably the least innocent of the
Innocents. He convened the Fourth Lateran Council, which forbade Jews from holding public office; forced them to pay extra
taxes and wear identifying clothing or badges; and forbade them
from marrying or having sexual relations with non-Jews. "So
deliberately worded to inflame public opinion were the Council
decrees," says historian Pinchas Lapide, "Jews were to be 'dis-
graced' and removed from the offices they had 'shamefully
assumed,' and so on—that they succeeded within one generation
in turning European Jewry into a race of pariahs, as remote from
society as India's untouchables."

Innocent IV (1243-1254). According to the *Oxford Dictionary of
Popes*, he "lowered the prestige of the papacy because he used his
spiritual powers constantly to raise money, buy friends, and injure
foes; he treated the endowments of the church as papal revenues
. . . [and] in 1252 he established the Inquisition as a permanent

Ann Glover, an elderly Irish Catholic widow living in Massachusetts,

institution in Italy." As if that weren't bad enough, he also issued the papal bull *Ad Exstirpanda*, which authorized the use of torture to obtain confessions . . . and permitted the burning of relapsed heretics at the stake.

Innocent VI (1352-1362). Was elected pope largely through his own dishonesty: When the College of Cardinals couldn't agree upon a successor to Pope Clement VI, each cardinal vowed to the others that if he were the one elected pope, he would share the papacy's power (and revenues) with the college. Innocent agreed only "in so far as it was not contrary to church law"—and then declared the agreement contrary to church law as soon as he became pope, keeping all the power and money for himself. (He was also a shameless nepotist—according to *The Lives and Times of the Roman Pontiffs*, "He was rather too much attached to his relatives, but it must be added that all those he favored deserved it.")

Innocent VIII (1484-1492). Was nicknamed "the Honest" because he was the first pope to publicly acknowledge his illegitimate children. Despite his nickname, he was a terrible pope—as the church's own *New Catholic Encyclopedia* put it, "The moral and political disorders of the time called for a pontiff of character and nobility; Innocent possessed neither." He became pope largely through bribing the other cardinals; drove the church nearly bankrupt by embroiling it in several Italian wars; and auctioned off curial posts to the highest bidder. Even so, Innocent was a man who knew his own weaknesses: When he died in 1492, he begged the cardinals to elect a pope "better than himself." (They didn't.)

Cardinal Innocenzo (Sixteenth century). *This* Innocenzo was no pope—he was the teenage lover of Pope Julius III, one of the few openly gay popes in church history. According to the *Oxford Dictionary of Popes*, Julius "created scandal by his infatuation with a fifteen-year-old youth, Innocenzo, picked up on the streets of Parma, whom he made his brother adopt and named a cardinal." (Cardinal Innocenzo was also keeper of the pope's pet ape.)

149

MORE CHRISTIAN CRITTERS

Here's another look at animals and their symbolic meanings.

Bees: Eloquence, hard work, order, and sweetness (because of the honey), virginity, and loyalty.

Peacocks: Pride, immortality, the all-seeing church (thanks to the "eyes" in the feathers).

Ravens: Evil (according to Jewish legend, it was originally white, but its feathers turned black when Noah sent it out from the Ark and it didn't return).

Pelicans: The crucifixion, Christ's suffering on the cross (from the ancient belief that the pelican mother pierces its breast and feeds its young with her own blood).

Scorpions: Evil (because of their fatal sting, Scorpions often appear on the flags and shields of the soldiers who helped crucify Christ; and are also used to symbolize Judas).

Snails: Sin and laziness (the early Christians thought that rather than look for tastier food, snails sucked the mud as they slithered over it).

Seashells: Religious pilgrimages.

Spiders: Misers and the devil (they feed on the blood of insects that they catch in their webs).

Cobwebs: Human frailty.

Whales: The devil (early sailors thought its immense bulk could be mistaken for an island—and that they would drown if they anchored their ships to it).

Open Mouth of a Whale: The gates of hell.

Eagles: The resurrection (from the ancient belief that the eagle replaced its feathers by flying close to the sun and then diving into the sea).

Catholics over 14 are still obliged to abstain from meat on Ash Wednesday, the Fridays

Giraffes: No particular meaning (but a popular subject of Renaissance art, since they were so funny looking).

Fish: Christ (reason: The five letters of *ΙΧΘΥΣ*, the Greek word for "fish," are also the first letters of the words "Jesus Christ God's Son Savior").

Camels: Temperance and sobriety (they don't drink very much); also royalty and wealth.

Centaurs (a man's torso on a horse's body): Adultery, savage passions, wickedness, and heresy.

Dogs: Watchfulness, fidelity (often shown at the feet or in the lap of a married woman).

Partridges: Truth, the church . . . or deceit, theft, and the devil.

Rams: Christ (since they too are leaders of the herd).

Lambs: Christ (the lamb is one of the few animals that is regularly depicted with a halo).

Goats: The damned on Judgment Day (reason: Just as shepherds separate the sheep from the goats, so will God separate the holy from sinners).

✠ ✠ ✠

HOLY SPIRITS

Looking for a party punch with a religious motif? Here are two recipes from My Nameday: Come for Dessert, *a cookbook the Benedictines published in 1962. Try 'em—you'll like 'em!*

Papst (Pope Punch). "Rub several lumps of sugar on half the rind of an orange; place it in a bowl. Add an orange cut in very thin slices, a small piece of cinnamon stick, and a clove or two. Add a bottle of Tokay wine; steep for 24 hours. . . . Serve on the feast-day of a pope."

Bishop Wine. "Heat to the boiling point a bottle of red Burgundy, 1 cup of sugar, one quarter teaspoon of cinnamon, and the grated rind of an orange. Serve hot."

of Lent, and Good Friday. (Sauces, meat gravy, and soup flavored with meat are O.K.)

KNOW YOUR BIBLE(S)

You've heard of the King James Version, the Revised Standard Version, and the New Revised Standard Version. Ever wondered why there are so many different versions in the first place? Here's an explanation, as well as a look at some versions you've probably never heard of:

I N THE BEGINNING

Even by nonreligious standards, the Bible and its various translations are the most significant written works the Western world has ever produced. They are mileposts by which historians measure the progress of European civilization: The Gutenberg Bible (c. 1455), for example, was the first book ever printed on a movable type printing press; Martin Luther's 1534 German translation is considered the cradle of the modern German language; and the King James Version of 1611 has been described as "the noblest monument of English prose," superior even to the works of William Shakespeare.

No one knows how many Bibles have been distributed over the centuries, but the number easily exceeds 100 million copies—by far the most popular book ever printed. So far the Bible has been translated into more than 260 different languages, including more than twenty different English versions, most of which are still in print. If there's one thing all of these different editions and translations demonstrate, it's that as spoken languages continue to evolve, the Bible needs to be updated regularly so that it remains accurate, understandable, and relevant to the people who read them. Here's a look at some of the most important, most popular, and most unusual updates ever produced:

THE CLASSICS

The Vulgate Bible (405). Translated by Saint Jerome (c. 342-420), the first person to translate into Latin the ancient Greek and Hebrew texts that make up the Bible. His version was named

Pope John Paul II makes the sign of the cross before he jumps in his swimming pool.

the "Vulgate" Bible because Latin was the language of the *vulgar* or common people, as opposed to Greek, the language of the upper classes and the nobility. The Vulgate is still in use today.

The Wycliffe Bible (1384). Shortly before his death, the English religious reformer John Wycliffe translated the Vulgate Bible into English. The only problem: The Catholic Church *forbade* English translations and denounced the translation as heretical. Wycliffe died before the church got its hands on him, but in 1415 the Council of Constance ordered his body dug up, burned, and thrown into a river.

The Tyndale Bible (1526). William Tyndale, an English Protestant reformer, published the first English translation of the Bible taken directly from the ancient Hebrew and Greek texts. It too was condemned by the church. In 1535 Tyndale was arrested on charges of "willfully perverting the meaning of the Scriptures"; a year later he was strangled and burned at the stake. (The first *approved* English translation, the Douay-Rheims Bible, was finally published in 1582.)

The King James Bible (1616). Commissioned by England's King James I, who wanted an official English translation of the Bible for Protestant churches. It was translated from a sixteenth-century Greek text . . . which was later discovered to contain fourteen centuries' worth of copyists' errors. So in 1885 the Anglican Church published an update, the English Revised Version—and in 1901 released the American Standard Version, a special translation for U.S. Protestants. (*Its* revision, the *Revised* Standard Version, was published in 1946 . . . which in turn was followed by the *New* Revised Standard Version in 1989.)

ODDBALL BIBLES

The Geneva Bible (1560). Nicknamed "the Breeches Bible" because it was the first Bible to depict Adam and Eve wearing pants. Why? The editors thought Genesis 3:7 (the passage where

Adam and Eve "sewed fig leaves together and made themselves *aprons*") was too racy . . . so they dumped "aprons" and replaced it with "breeches."

Webster's Bible (1883). Published by Noah Webster, creator of *Webster's Dictionary*. He too thought the Bible was filled with smut: "Many words and phrases," he complained, "are so offensive, especially to females, as to create a reluctance in young persons to attend Bible classes and schools in which they are required to read passages which cannot be repeated without a blush." So he rewrote the entire Bible, removing the "filthiest" passages entirely and cleaning up the less offensive ones. Words such as "whore," "fornication," "teat," and "to give suck" gave way to milder expressions like "lewd woman," "lewdness," "breast," and "to nurse," the end result being a Bible that wasn't nearly as much fun to read as the one it replaced.

GOOD NEWS FOR MODERN MAN
Is the Bible becoming outdated—perhaps even irrelevant—in the 1990s? Not if these versions of the good book can help it:

The Black Bible Chronicles. In 1993 African American Family Press released *The Black Bible Chronicles: A Survival Manual for the Streets*, a street-language paraphrase of the first five books of the Old Testament. ("Thou shalt not steal" appears as "You shouldn't be takin' nothin' from your homeboys"; "Thou shalt not kill" translates "Don't waste nobody"; and "Thou shalt not commit adultery" emerges as "Don't mess around with someone else's ol' man or ol' lady.") The book was written by P. K. McCary, a Houston, Texas, Sunday school teacher who was having trouble reaching inner-city kids using standard Bible texts. "Over the years, I have found that kids just pick up on this language. For them, it's a kick. As my daughter would say, 'It's tight.' "

The Klingon Authorized Version. Ambrose Bierce once described faith as "belief without evidence in what is told by one

Q: What's the second-best selling book in history after the Bible?

who speaks without knowledge, of things without parallel." The folks at the Klingon Bible Translation Project are taking the concept one step further—they're translating the Bible into an imaginary language so that it can be read by a race of people who don't exist . . . except in the minds of *Star Trek* fans. Example translation: John 3:16 ("For God so loved the world, that he gave his only begotten Son, that whosoever believeth in him should not perish but have everlasting life") reads: "toH qo' muSHa'pu'qu'-mo' joH'a', wa' puqloDDaj nobpu' ghaH 'ej ghaHbaq Harchugh vay', vaj not Hegh ghaH, 'ach yIn jub ghajbeh ghaH."

When finished, the Klingon Authorized Version will prove two things: (1) That the word of God truly *is* universal; and (2) that *Star Trek* fans need to get out more often.

✢　　✢　　✢

BIBLE BOO-BOOS

• **The He Bible.** In the first printing of the King James Bible, the printers and proofreaders failed to catch a mistake in Ruth 3:15. Referring to Ruth's departure from Boaz, the passage reads, ". . . and *he* went into the city." The Bible became known as the He Bible.

• **The She Bible.** The printers got it right the second time around: the next printing read, ". . . and *she* went into the city," earning it the nickname the She Bible.

• **The Wicked Bible.** In 1631, two London printers left one word out of an official edition of the Bible. The mistake cost them three thousand pounds and nearly led to their imprisonment. The word was "not;" they left it out of the Seventh Commandment, which then told readers, "Thou shalt commit adultery." The book became known as the "Wicked Bible."

A: Dr. Benjamin Spock's *Common Sense Book of Baby and Child Care* (1946).

THEY LOST THAT LOVIN' FEELING

Come on, admit it: You occasionally suffer from sexual temptation. We all do . . . even the saints, believe it or not. Need help controlling those carnal urges? Here's how the saints kept theirs in check.

St. Benedict of Nursia: Moved to a cave to escape the immorality of those around him, but still suffered intense sexual temptation. Overcame it by rolling in a thorn bush that grew outside his cave.

St. Peter Damian: Whipped himself, wore an iron girdle, and when all else failed, jumped into thorn bushes.

St. Aloysius Gonzaga: Refused to be alone in the same room with *any* woman, even his mother—and slept on sharp chunks of wood.

St. Dominic Savio: No word on how this holy ten-year-old resisted his own sexual temptations, but he helped his schoolmates resist theirs by stealing their dirty pictures and destroying them.

St. Bernard of Clairvaux: Threw himself into half-frozen ponds. Also wrote lengthy commentaries on the biblical Song of Songs "to prove it was not about sex."

St. Jerome: Conquered visions of dancing maidens by "throwing himself in tears before a crucifix, beating his breast with a stone, and fleeing into the desert."

St. Gabriel Possenti: Wrapped himself in chains set with sharp points.

St. Francis of Assisi: Rolled naked in the snow . . . and jumped into thorn bushes.

St. Thomas Aquinas. When his brothers brought a young maiden to his chambers he chased her out with a red-hot poker (from the fireplace).

Q: What's the proper way to say the rosary—clockwise, or counterclockwise?

HOLIER THAN THOU

Some saints are remembered for being holy . . . others are remembered for being really holy. Take these folks, for example:

Saint Martin de Porres (1579-1639). Offered to sell himself into slavery when his Dominican monastery was in a financial pinch (he was half black). The Dominicans declined the offer and nicknamed him "father of charity"; he preferred the name "mulatto dog." According to one source, Saint Martin's charity "extended to animals, even vermin. He protected them, and even excused the wrongdoings of rats, saying they were 'poorly fed.' Sometimes he even allowed mosquitoes to bite him." (He later died from a fever . . . which he may have gotten from a mosquito bite.)

Saint Simeon Salus (c. 589). Was nicknamed *Salus* ("the Mad") for "his practice of allowing himself to be considered an idiot out of humility." His fame may have gone to his head—according to the Penguin *Dictionary of Saints*, "So outrageous did his conduct become . . . that it seems likely that he was at times really out of his mind."

Saint Joseph of Cupertino (1603-1663). Took religious austerity to extremes: After he became a Franciscan monk in 1628, Joseph mailed his underwear back to his mother "because his habit was all he needed." He wore *that* for two years without removing it.

Saint Fursey (c. 600). Spoke to his parents from the womb before he was born—a talent credited to a number of saints, including Saint Isaac, "who made his voice heard three times in one day."

Saint Rumwold (c. 600). Died three days after he was born, but used his time on earth wisely—"he not only professed his faith in such a way as to be understood by all the bystanders, but also preached a long sermon to his parents and relatives before dying."

A: It doesn't matter.

Saint Catherine of Sweden (1331-1381). Another holy infant: Abstained from breast feeding for twenty-four hours anytime her parents had sex.

Saint Lawrence (258). When Church officials opened his tomb four hundred years after his death to inter Saint Stephen's body next to him, Lawrence "moved over to make room for the corpse." Since then he has been known as "the courteous Spaniard."

Saint Eleutherius (c. 135). Preached a sermon to animals . . . and was so impressive that "the listening beasts, not being able to praise God with the voice, all lifted up the right foot in worship."

Saint Antony of Padua (1195-1231). Another animal charmer. Was so eloquent that when he preached to some fishes, they "rose out of the water to hear him."

Saint Ambrose (334-397). Not long after he was born, "a swarm of bees alighted on his mouth, thus foretelling his future eloquence."

Saint Euphemia (c. 303). "When thrown to the wild animals in the arena, she was worshiped, rather than eaten, by a bear."

Saint Peter (c. 64). Asked to be crucified upside down "so that his head would be lower than his Master's." His executioners obliged; according to legend it took Peter a long time to die in this position, but he made the most of it . . . by delivering a lecture on the symbolic importance of the crucifixion.

Saint James the Less (c. 62). Spent so much time praying that "his knees became as hard as a camel's."

✛ ✛ ✛

. . . LAST BUT NOT LEAST
St. Yves (1303). Was a lawyer "but not a thief, which astonished everyone."

According to one 15th-century estimate, 18,000 priests, 346 "clowns, dancers, and

HOW TO BAPTIZE
IN AN EMERGENCY

Can heathens baptize in a crisis? What if someone is trapped under a rock—can you baptize their feet if their head is out of reach? Can you baptize someone with Diet Coke if no water is available? The Baltimore Catechism tackles these and other pressing questions.

Q 631. Is Baptism necessary to salvation?
A. Baptism is necessary to salvation, because without it we cannot enter the kingdom of heaven.

Q. 633. Who can administer Baptism?
A. A priest is the ordinary minister of Baptism; but . . . any person of either sex who has reached the use of reason can baptize in case of necessity. . . . A man, if he be present and knows how to administer the Sacrament, should baptize in preference to a woman.

Q. 638. How is Baptism given?
A. Whoever baptizes should pour water on the head of the person to be baptized, and say, while pouring the water: "I baptize thee in the name of the Father, and of the Son, and of the Holy Ghost."

Q. 639. If water cannot be had, in case of necessity, may any other liquid be used for Baptism?
A. If water cannot be had, in case of necessity or in any case, no other liquid can be used, and the baptism cannot be given.

Q. 640. If it is impossible, in case of necessity, to reach the head, may the water be poured on any other part of the body?
A. If it is impossible, in case of necessity, to reach the head, the water should be poured on whatever part of the body can be reached; but then the baptism must be given conditionally; that is,

jugglers," and "1,500 harlots" attended the Council of Constance from 1414 to 1418.

before pronouncing the words of baptism, you must say: "If I can baptize thee in this way, I baptize thee in the name of the Father," etc. If the head can afterward be reached, the water must be poured on the head and the baptism repeated conditionally by saying: "If you are not already baptized, I baptize thee in the name," etc.

Q. 632. Where will persons go who—such as infants—have not committed actual sin and who, through no fault of theirs, die without Baptism?
A. . . . It is the common belief they will go to some place similar to Limbo, where they will be free from suffering, though deprived of the happiness of heaven.

Q. 642. Is it wrong to defer the baptism of an infant?
A. It is wrong to defer the baptism of an infant, because we thereby expose the child to the danger of dying without the Sacrament.

Q. 643. Can we baptize a child against the wishes of its parents?
A. We cannot baptize a child against the wishes of its parents; and if the parents are not Catholics, they must not only consent to the baptism, but also agree to bring the child up in the Catholic religion. But if a child is surely dying, we may baptize it without either the consent or permission of its parents.

. . . ONE LAST QUESTION
Q. 659. What names should never be given in Baptism?
A. These and similar names should never be given in Baptism: (1) The names of noted unbelievers, heretics or enemies of religion and virtue; (2) the names of heathen gods, and (3) nicknames.

"[Woman is] the devil's gateway . . . a scorpion's dart."   —Saint Jerome (342-420)

TRUE CONFESSIONS

*Did you think you had to be perfect to become a saint? Think again.
By his own admission, Saint Augustine was a sex maniac and sinner
extraordinaire before converting to Christianity at the age of thirty-
two. Here are some excerpts from his book, Confessions:*

LITTLE SINS

Kid Stuff

"I was even troublesome to the people whom I set out to please.
Many and many a time I lied to my tutor, my masters, and my parents, and deceived them because I wanted to play games or watch
some futile show.

"I even stole from my parents' larder and from their table, either
from greed or to get something to give to other boys in exchange
for their favorite toys. . . . And in the games I played with them I
often cheated in order to come off the better, simply because a
vain desire to win had got the better of me."

BIG SINS

Lust

"As a youth I had been woefully at fault, particularly in early ado-
lescence. I had prayed to you for chastity and said, 'Give me
chastity and continence, but not yet.' For I was afraid that you
would answer my prayer at once and cure me too soon of the disease of lust, which I wanted satisfied, not quelled."

More Lust

"Bodily desire, like a morass, and adolescent sex welling up within
me exuded mists which clouded over and obscured my heart.
. . . Love and lust together seethed within me. In my tender youth
they swept me away over the precipice of my body's appetites and
plunged me into the whirlpool of sin. . . . I was tossed and spilled,
floundering in the sea of my own fornication."

Fast food: You can eat one full meal and two small meals (no meat) on fast days.

Lust and Public Nudity
"The brambles of my lust grew high above my head and there was no one to root them out, certainly not my father. One day at the public baths he saw the signs of active virility coming to life in me and this was enough to make him relish the thought of having grandchildren."

Lust and Politics
"Where was I then and how far was I banished from the bliss of your house in the sixteenth year of my life? This was the age at which the frenzy gripped me and I surrendered myself entirely to lust. . . . My family made no effort to save me from my fall by marriage. Their only concern was that I should learn how to make a good speech and how to persuade others by my word."

Lust During Mass
"I defied you even so far as to relish the thought of lust, and *gratify* it, too, within the walls of your church during the celebration of your mysteries. For such a deed I deserved to pluck the fruit of death."

Living in Sin
"In those days I lived with a woman, not my lawful wedded wife, but a mistress whom I had chosen for no special reason but that my restless passions had alighted on her. But she was the only one and I was faithful to her."

Still More Lust
"I went to Carthage, where I found myself in the midst of a cauldron of lust. . . . Was it any wonder that I, the unhappy sheep who strayed from your flock, impatient of your shepherding, became infected with a loathsome mange? . . . Where the fingers scratch, the skin becomes inflamed. It swells and festers with hideous pus."

. . . One Last Sin
"Besides these pursuits, I was also studying for the law."

Q: What is the pope's official salary, in U.S. dollars?

EVEN MORE CATHOLIC WORD ORIGINS

More Catholic origins of everyday words . . . including a few dirty ones.

BEG

Meaning: To ask people for money or something else of value.

Background: In the twelfth century Lambert de Begue, an Italian cleric, founded an order of *mendicant* monks (friars who lived entirely on donations they solicited from the public). His name—pronounced *beg*—eventually became synonymous with the way his followers made their living.

PUMPERNICKEL

Meaning: A coarse rye bread that originated in Germany.

Background: If you hate the way pumpernickel tastes today, take heart in the fact that it doesn't taste as bad as it did centuries ago, when Catholic bakers invented it in the Westphalia region of Germany. The 1756 book *A Grand Tour of Germany* described it as bread "of the very coarsest kind, ill baked, and as black as coal, for they never sift their flour." Locals joked that it was so difficult to digest that it even the devil himself got gas when he ate it; in fact, the word "pumpernickel" is a play on the German words *pumpern* ("break wind") and *Nickel* ("Old Nick the devil").

PANTS

Meaning: Trousers.

Background: Saint Pantaleone was a Christian physician who was beheaded in the fourth century during the reign of the Roman emperor Diocletian. His name is strikingly similar to the battle cry of the city of Venice, *Piante Lione!* ("Plant the Lion!"), so much so

A: $0.

that Venetians made him a patron saint . . . and often painted him wearing the flared trousers that were popular in the city. By the eighteenth century the garment was so closely associated with him that they were known as *pantaleones*, a term that Americans abbreviated to "pants."

LOBBY

Meaning: The open public area of an office building or hotel.

Background: In the Middle Ages when monks were the only educated people in many towns, illiterate peasants depended on them for help with letter writing, legal aid, and other services. Many monasteries built vine-covered walkways (called *lobias* in German) to accommodate the people waiting for assistance. The word lobia was adopted into the English language as the word "lobby," which eventually came to mean any public waiting area.

DUMBBELLS

Meaning: A small weight used in exercise.

Background: Church bells were an important part of life during the Middle Ages, and ringing them properly required a surprising amount of skill. But it was almost impossible for beginners to practice without driving townspeople crazy from the noise . . . at least until someone invented a set of *dumb* bells—weights suspended from ropes—that worked just like the real bells, except that they didn't make any noise. Working with the heavy weights developed the user's bell-ringing skills *and* his physique, so much so that *non*-bellringers began using them to get into shape. The name "dumbbell" came to apply to any set of weights that helped you get in shape . . . whether or not they had anything to do with bells.

DUNCE

Meaning: A stupid person.

Background: John Duns Scotus was a brilliant thirteenth-century

Between 1860 and 1871, the area of Italy ruled by the pope shrank from 16,000 sq.

theologian, but by the sixteenth century many of his ideas had fallen out of favor. The Dutch scholar Erasmus denounced him so frequently and persuasively that Dun's name—re-spelled "dunce"—literally became synonymous with stupidity.

FRANCHISE

Meaning: A privilege or right that a government or business gives to an individual or other group. It comes from the Old French word *francher*, which means "to free."

Background: The Catholic Church helped popularize the term during the Middle Ages, when it granted franchises to individuals that gave them the right to collect taxes for the pope and keep a percentage for themselves.

FILBERT

Meaning: Another name for a hazelnut.

Background: One variety of French hazelnuts ripens on or around August 20, Saint Philibert's Day. The French nicknamed them *noix de filbert*, a name the English later shortened to "filberts."

GOBLINS

Meaning: An evil monster or spirit.

Background: In 1435 two Paris fabric makers named Gilles and Jehan Gobelin invented a dye that produced a brighter shade of red cloth than had ever been possible before. France was a deeply religious Catholic country at the time, not to mention crawling with fabric makers who envied the Gobelin's innovation. Soon after their product hit the market, rumors began spreading that they had sold their souls to the devil to learn how to make the blood red cloth. They grew so rampant that the name Gobelin became synonymous with evil . . . and even became the name of an imaginary evil creature, the *goblin*.

. . . LAST BUT NOT LEAST: *DIRTY WORD ORIGINS*

SEX. The word "sex" entered the English language in 1384 when John Wycliffe, an English religious reformer, translated the Bible into English for the first time: "Of alle thingis havynge sowle of ony flesh, two thow shalt brynge into the ark, that maal sex and femaal lyven with thee."

THE "F-WORD." No kidding: The most famous obscenity of all first appears in print in a fifteenth-century poem accusing some English monks of adultery. According to *The American Heritage Dictionary*, "The poem, composed in a mixture of Latin and English, satirizes the Carmelite Friars of Cambridge, England, with the title taken from the first words of the poem, 'Flen, flyys, and freris,' that is, 'fleas, flies, and friars.' The line that contains f___ . . . reads in translation, '[The friars] are not in heaven because they f___ wives of Ely [a town near Cambridge].' "

✢ ✢ ✢

. . . PISTOL-PACKIN' PADRE

In 1987 the Citizens Committee for the Right to Keep and Bear Arms asked the Vatican to name Gabriel Possenti, a nineteenth-century Italian priest, the patron of handgunners. Reason: In 1859 he disarmed some mutinous soldiers by grabbing one of their guns and shooting a lizard in the head—thus proving in the eyes of the committee that pistols, "in the hands of a person committed in heart, mind and soul to Almighty God, may be used to bring about practical good here on earth." (The Vatican denied the request.)

Candy trivia: According to one popular legend, the crown

MORE CHURCH LINGO

More unusual words and phrases used by the clergy.

Obreption: A falsehood used to gain a religious favor, dispensation, or privilege.

Cenobite: Another word for monk.

Thurifer: The person who carries the *thurible* or incense burner during Mass.

Hymnody: Religious lyric poetry.

Catechumen: A person receiving formal religious instruction.

Black Pope: The nickname of the father general of the Society of Jesus (Jesuits).

Proxy Marriage: A marriage in which the bride or groom (or both) are not present at the wedding ceremony and are represented by a stand-in or *proxy*. (Special permission is required.)

Lady Chapel: A chapel dedicated to the Virgin Mary.

Putative Father: From the Latin word *puto*, which means "think" or "suppose." It's used to describe the Virgin Mary's husband Joseph, because "his friends thought he was the carnal father of Christ."

Putative Marriage: A marriage that is invalid because of some defect that is grounds for annulment.

Cowl: A monk's hood.

Pro-Cathedral: A church that is used as a temporary substitute for a permanent cathedral.

Quasi-Parish: A parish that has not yet become a full-fledged parish.

Licit: Something that does not break religious law.

Illicit: Something that *does*.

Sodality: An organization that promotes pious or charitable acts.

of thorns was made from branches of the jujube plant.

ODD JOBS

*Many of the Church's patron saints seem pretty conventional
. . . until you look at why certain saints were selected
for their specialties:*

Saint John (6-104).
Specialty: Candlemakers.
Reason: He was boiled in oil.

Saint John Nepomucene (1340-1393)
Specialty: Bridge builders and confessors.
Reason: He was tortured and thrown off a bridge (with his heels
tied to his forehead) after he refused to reveal the confessional
secrets of the Queen of Bohemia to her husband, King Wenceslaus
IV. He is often depicted holding a finger to his lips, with his lips
padlocked shut . . . or being thrown off of a bridge.

Saint Apollonia (c. 249)
Specialty: Dentists.
Reason: An angry mob of heathens plucked her teeth out with
pincers after she refused to renounce Christianity. She is often
depicted strapped to a board, with one executioner pulling her
hair while another yanks out her teeth.

Saint Onuphrius (400).
Specialty: Weavers.
Reason: No one knows for sure—he never wore any clothes.
During the sixty years he lived alone in the desert, Onuphrius
wore nothing but a garland of leaves that hid his private parts.
(One theory: The weavers were joking when they picked him.)

Saint Bartholomew (first century).
Speciality: *Tanners*—people who work with animal skins.

In one public audience early in his papacy, Pope John Paul II told the audience

Reason: His executioners skinned him alive and then chopped his head off. He is often depicted with strips of his flesh hanging off of his arm, or with a human pelt draped over his forearm.

Saint Blaise (316).
Specialty: Wool combers.
Reason: His executioners literally shredded his flesh using the spiked metal combs that are used to prepare wool to be woven.

Saint Genesius the Comedian (Third Century).
Specialty: Actors.
Reason: Genesius was a pagan actor who converted to Christianity halfway through a performance in a play mocking Christian baptisms. After his conversion he refused to finish the scene, and the performance was cancelled. (Bad luck: The Roman emperor Diocletian was in the audience . . . and was so angry at the cancellation that he had Genesius beheaded.)

Saint Matrona (date unknown).
Specialty: People suffering from dysentery.
Reason: Who knows? When she contracted dysentery, a voice told her that if she went to Italy she would be cured. So she went to Italy . . . and died from the disease shortly after she got there.

Saint Harvey (Sixth century).
Specialty: Eye trouble.
Background: Another strange choice—Harvey was born blind, remained blind for the rest of his life, died blind . . . and is not credited with curing any eye diseases during his lifetime.

Saint Dorothy (c. 303).
Specialty: Brides.
Reason: Yet another mysterious choice. Dorothy never married—and when she turned down a Roman official's proposal, he had her jailed, starved, boiled in oil, stretched over a fire, and beheaded.

that married couples would be reunited in heaven . . . but they wouldn't have sex.

Saint Martha (who may have been Mary Magdalene's sister).
Specialty: Dieticians.
Reason: Once when Jesus was visiting her house, Martha yelled at Mary Magdalene for not helping prepare the meal (she was too busy talking to Jesus). Martha's enthusiasm for cooking—even to the extent of pulling Mary Magdalene away from a conversation with Christ—encouraged dieticians to pick her as their patron.

Saint Julian the Hospitaler (date unknown).
Specialty: Hotel keepers.
Reason: One night when he came home from a trip, Saint Julian found a man and woman sleeping in his bed and assumed his wife was cheating on him. Without double-checking, he drew his sword and slew the two, only to find out afterwards that they were his parents, who had dropped in for a visit and were napping in the master bedroom while his wife was at Mass. Overcome with guilt, Julian spent the rest of his life running a hotel and hospital for the poor. (Note: He is also the patron saint of travelers and circus performers—who travel a lot).

Saint Martin de Porres (1579-1639).
Specialty: Italian barbers.
Reason: He was a barber before he became a Dominican monk . . . and continued giving haircuts after joining the order.

Saint Acacius (c. 251).
Specialty: Headaches.
Reason: His executioners crowned him with thorns before they killed him.

Saint Margaret (date unknown).
Speciality: Kidney disease, childbirth, and abdominal pains.
Reason: She escaped from the stomach of a dragon by bursting open its chest with a crucifix.

Pope John XXIII made St. Bona the patron saint of stewardesses on March 2, 1962.

GET PROFESSIONAL HELP

Having trouble at work? If you're a member of any of the professions listed below, count your blessings—you have a patron saint.

Soap boilers: St. Florian

Chicken farmers: St. Brigid

Grave diggers: St. Antony the Great

Pencil makers: St. Thomas Aquinas

Fishmongers: St. Andrew the Apostle

Ribbon makers: St. Mary

Old clothes dealers: St. Anne

Playing card makers: St. Balthasar

Thieves: St. Dismas

Fruit dealers: St. Christopher

Rope makers: St. Paul

Prison guards: St. Adrian

Advertisers: St. Bernardino of Siena

Glove makers: St. Mary Magdalene

Net makers: St. Peter

Women "who have formerly lived in sin": St. Mary of Egypt

Tax collectors and security guards: St. Matthew

Television workers: St. Clare

Nail makers: St. Cloud

Pin makers: St. Sebastian

Knife makers: St. Catherine of Alexandria

Ammunition workers: St. Barbara (her executioner was struck by lightning)

Arms dealers: St. Adrian

Cattle dealers: St. Theodard

Cattle breeders: St. Mark

Altar boys: St. John Berchmans

Astronauts: St. Joseph of Cupertino (he levitated in front of the pope)

First pope to canonize a saint: John XV in 993.

KINKY SECTS

Here's a look at some of the weirdest heretics
ever to split from the Roman Catholic Church.

THE OPHITES
An early Gnostic Christian sect that believed Adam and Eve's
eating of the forbidden fruit was a *good* thing, since it brought
knowledge of good and evil into the world. To them the snake
was the hero in the story, so much so that they "required that the
bread of the Eucharist be licked by serpents before serving it to
communicants."

THE CATAPHRYGIANS
An early separatist movement led by a man named Montanus.
Rather than join their hands to pray, members "put their index
and middle fingers into their nostrils" and prayed in that position.

THE ADAMITES
An obscure, second-century Christian sect whose members
"renounced marriage, shed their clothing, and indulged in a variety of pagan and lustful practices."

THE OTHER ADAMITES
An obscure fifteenth-century Christian sect whose members
"renounced marriage, shed their clothing, and indulged in a variety of pagan and lustful practices." Unlike the first bunch, these
Adamites were led by a Frenchman named Picard, who proclaimed himself to be the second incarnation of Adam. They were
annihilated by the Hussites (another band of heretics) in 1421.

SAINT PETER DAMIAN'S LAY FLAGELLANTS
Clergy self-mortification dates back to the oldest days of the
church; but it wasn't until the eleventh century that a religious

Did Jesus have a beard . . . or blue eyes? Nobody knows for sure—no one

hermit named Saint Peter Damian organized groups of *lay* flagellants, people who marched through the towns of Europe whipping themselves and chanting as they walked. The Black Death of the mid-fourteenth century made the movement even more popular; according to one source, by 1350 "Europe was criss-crossed from end to end by hordes of desperate men, women, and children scourging themselves for the Glory of God."

THE LOTHARDI
An obscure fourteenth-century offshoot of the Russian Orthodox Church, which split from Roman Catholicism in 1056. The Lothardi believed in living morally strict lives . . . at least when they were *above* ground. But according to the *People's Almanac*, "once they were at least 27 inches below ground, everything changed. Hence, all their meetings were held in subterranean caves and were riotous orgies."

THE MULTIPLICANTS
A heretical, eighteenth-century French cult best known for its twenty-four-hour marriages (which the newlyweds consummated on the altar during the wedding) and its devotion to group sex, innovations that reduced the divorce rate considerably. French authorities were not amused: They raided the sect in 1723, hanged its leaders, and forced the women into nunneries.

✠ ✠ ✠

. . . FOOT NOTE
What is Saint Hedwig (1174-1243) remembered for? Among other things, the extreme (some say downright bizarre) ways in which she humbled herself before her fellow nuns. A Bavarian housewife and mother of seven children, Hedwig entered a convent when her husband died after twenty-five years of marriage. Her modesty took many forms, including kissing chair seats and "washing the feet of the nuns, then drinking the dirty water."

who knew Jesus bothered to write down what he looked like.

A SAINT SAID THAT?

If you're upset that the church teaches that popes are infallible in matters of faith and morals, just be glad they aren't saying the same thing about saints:

"If babies are innocent, it is not for lack of will to do harm but for lack of strength."

—Saint Augustine (354-430)

Christian soldiers "are to wage the war of Christ their master without fearing that they sin in killing their enemies or of being lost if they are themselves killed, since when they give or receive the death blow, they are guilty of no crime, but all is to their glory. If they kill, it is to the profit of Christ; if they die, it is to their own."

—Saint Bernard (1090-1153)

"Pleasure can never be without sin."

—Pope Saint Gregory (540-604)

"Laughter does not seem to be a sin, but it leads to sin."

—Saint John Chrysostom (347-407)

"Little children who have begun to live in their mothers' womb and have there died, or who, having just been born, have passed away from the world without the sacrament of holy baptism . . . must be punished by the eternal torture of undying fire."

—Saint Fulgentius (467-533)

"We should always be disposed to believe that which appears white is really black, if the hierarchy of the Church so decides."

—Saint Ignatius of Loyola (1491-1556)

In 1701 the State of New Jersey granted religous freedom to everyone except "papists."

"Of all the Roman ladies, only one had the power to tempt me, and that one was Paula. She mourned and she fasted. She was squalid with dirt; here eyes were dim from weeping. . . . The Psalms were her only songs; the gospel her only speech; continence her one indulgence; fasting her staple of life."

—Saint Jerome

"Do away with harlots, and the world will be convulsed with lust."

—Saint Augustine

"I am aware that some have laid it down that the virgins of Christ must not bathe with eunuchs or married women, because the former still have the minds of men and the latter present the ugly spectre of swollen bellies. But for my part I say that mature girls must not bathe at all, because they ought to blush to see themselves naked."

—Saint Jerome (342-420)

✠ ✠ ✠

THE COUNCIL OF TRENT (1545-1563) EXPLAINED

"The Council of Trent . . . addressed such 'prevalent abuses' as priests extorting stipends for private Masses . . . the selling of 'bargain' Masses; and the practice of several Masses being conducted in the same church at the same time. . . . In addition, the Council condemned such 'less prevalent' abuses as priests elevating the chalice by placing it on their heads; dead bodies being laid on the altar during Mass; hunters coming to the Lord's Supper with hawks and dogs; and processions of the Blessed Sacrament from different churches crossing and breaking into brawls."

—Everything You Always Wanted to Know About the Catholic Church but Were Afraid to Ask for Fear of Excommunication, by Paul L. Williams (1989)

Every pope since Sergius IV (1009-1012) has changed his name.

TO ERR IS HUMAN . . .

In the nearly two thousand years since the dawn of Christianity, the stories of the saints told and retold, and their images painted and repainted more times than anyone knows—and more than once in the process, somebody got the details just a little bit wrong:

OOPS!
Keeping track of the saints has never been an easy job. During the Middle Ages, for example, there were more than twenty-five thousand saints to chose from; more than any Christian (the vast majority of whom were illiterate) could handle. One way the church and its artisans made life a little easier was by depicting most saints with symbols or *attributes* taken from their life stories, which gave the faithful something they could use as identifying marks. (Saint Peter, for example, is usually depicted holding *keys:* as the first pope of the Catholic Church, he holds the keys to heaven.)

The system was simple and effective—anytime someone saw a picture of a saint holding keys, they knew it was Saint Peter. But it wasn't perfect: Some symbols were harder to make out than others, and over the centuries their meaning was forgotten. New generations would look at the art, misinterpret the attribute, and in a number of cases create entirely new legends around what they thought the symbol was supposed to be.

. . . And that wasn't the only kind of slip-up that could befall a saint: Errors as tiny as a misspelled name or a mistranslated word in their biography could give rise to a brand new legend completely at odds with their original life story. Some examples:

THE VIRGIN MARY
The Scene: In some depictions of the Annunciation (when the Angel Gabriel *announces* to the Virgin Mary that she is going to

Saint Fiacre is the patron saint of hemorrhoid sufferers.

give birth to Jesus), the Holy Spirit is portrayed as a dove hovering above Mary's ear.

The Mistake: "This caused some commentators," says J. C. Metford, author of *The Dictionary of Christian Lore and Legend*, "to explain that Mary conceived through her ear, [thus] preserving her virginity intact."

SAINT ELMO (third century)

The Scene: The patron saint of sailors, Elmo is often shown standing next to a *windlass*, a cranklike device used on boats.

The Mistake: At some point in the Middle Ages, artists mistook the windlass for a torture device—and began painting Elmo with his intestines pulled out and wound around it. Largely because of this mistake, Saint Elmo is one of the saints commonly invoked against cramps, labor pains, and stomachaches.

SAINT AGATHA (251)

The Scene: According to legend, a spurned suitor cut off Agatha's breasts after she refused to sleep with him. Saint Peter appeared to her in a vision and reattached them; even so, she is often shown carrying her breasts on a silver platter.

The Mistake: In some parts of Europe the breasts were mistaken for bells . . . and Agatha became the patron saint of bell makers and bell ringers. In other places they were mistaken for loaves of bread, "thus originating a rite of blessing bread on her feast day."

SAINT BARTHOLOMEW (c. 50)

The Scene: One of the twelve apostles, Bartholomew was flayed alive by a heathen king. His attribute is a flaying knife.

The Mistake: Some medieval cheese merchants mistook the knife for a cheese slicer . . . which is how Saint Bart became the patron saint of cheese makers.

SAINT VIVIANA (363)

The Problem: Her name means "full of life" in Latin (*vivo*); but the medieval Spanish misinterpreted her name as *Bibiana*, "full of drink" (*bibo*).

What Happened: She became the patron saint invoked against hangovers.

SAINT LAWRENCE (257)

The Legend: When a greedy Roman prefect ordered Lawrence, the archdeacon of Rome, to hand over all of the church's treasures, he asked for three days to do it. Three days later he showed up at the prefect's palace—along with thousands of orphans, widows, lepers, blind people, and the lame. He presented them to the prefect and said: "Here are the Church's treasures." The prefect must have had something else in mind, because when he saw the crowd he ordered Lawrence scourged, clubbed, branded, stretched on the rack, torn with metal hooks . . . and then had him roasted alive over a gridiron. During the roasting Lawrence supposedly said to his executioners, "Turn me over, I'm done on this side." They did . . . and just before he died told them, "It is cooked enough. You may eat." (They didn't.)

The Mistake: Some scholars say the incident never happened, arguing that such a death would have been very unusual . . . and that *passus est*, the Latin phrase for "he suffered," is only one letter different from *assus est*, the phrase for "he was roasted." They speculate that at some point in history a copyist forgot to p.

MOSES (Thirteenth century B.C.)

Okay, so Moses isn't a Catholic saint . . . but he is the victim of one of the most egregious mistakes in Catholic Church history, thanks to an error made when the Old Testament was translated from Hebrew to Latin. What happened: Scholars confused the Hebrew phrase for "rays of light" with the word for "horn" (in Hebrew the phrase can mean *either* horns or rays)—and in one

Mass Hysteria: Four whites were hanged and 11 blacks burned at the stake in

critical passage, changed the sentence from Moses having horns *of light* shining on his head to having *horns* on his head. The error is believed to be at least partially responsible for the anti-Semitic belief that Jews, like the devil, literally have horns sticking out of their foreheads. Even Michelangelo believed it—in 1513 he sculpted a horned statue of Moses for the tomb of Pope Julius III; it is still visible in Rome today.

✠ ✠ ✠

...WHAT ARE YOU AFRAID OF?
Here are some church-related fears you may have experienced in the past:

Bogyphobia: Fear of evil spirits

Hagiophobia: Fear of saints and holy people

Hamartophobia: Fear of sins or errors

Homilophobia: Fear of sermons

Macrophobia: Fear of long waits

Oenophobia: Fear of wine

Papaphobia: Fear of the pope or the papacy

Peccatiphobia: Fear of sinning

Staurophobia: Fear of crosses or crucifixes

Stygiophobia: Fear of hell

Teleophobia: Fear of religious ceremonies (not to be confused with **telephonophobia**—fear of using the telephone)

Theophobia: Fear of God

1741 as punishment for an alleged "popish plot" to burn the city of New York.

MORE HOLY HELPERS

Does your stomach hurt? Is a mad dog lapping at your heels? Can't shake that nagging cough? If nothing else works, you can pray to the patron saints associated with the problems listed below. Good Luck!

Headaches: Saint Acacius

Fever, inflammation, kidney disease, and "temptations of the devil": Saint Benedict

Storms, hail, toothaches . . . and sudden death: Saint Christopher

Fever and snakes: Saint Dominic of Sora

Hail and snakes: Saint Paul

Bad knees, cattle diseases, and bubonic plague: Saint Roch

Leg diseases, rats, and mice: Saint Servatus

Eye diseases, dysentery, and "hemorrhages in general": Saint Lucy

Worms: Saint Benen

Hernias: Saint Cathal

Belgians with hernias: Saint Gomer

Diseased tongues: Saint Catherine of Alexandria

Bruises: Saint Amalburga

Rabies and demonic possession: Saint Denis

Carbunkles: Saint Cloud

Fly bites: Saint Mark

Syphilis: Saint George

Lameness, insanity, sterility, and epilepsy: Saint Giles

Wounds: Saint Aldegund

Ruptures: Saint Osmund

Paralysis and apoplexy: Saint Wolfgang

"Gravel in the urine": Saint Drogo

✠ ✠ ✠

. . . IF ALL ELSE FAILS: Saint Ursula, "invoked for a good death"

There are more than 700 cars in the Vatican City motor pool.

A (CARNAL) SIN BY ANY OTHER NAME. . .

In the old days it was called "onanism," "self-satisfaction"—even "self-abuse" and was considered a very serious sin. It's still a sin today, even though most theologians agree that it's an insignificant one. Here's some slightly dated advice on how to deal with it.

THE EXPERTS SPEAK
"Young priests rarely fail to be amazed . . . when they find so many obviously capable, good-intentioned, conscientious young men functioning with normal, healthy, moral resoluteness in every area but this. . . .

"The [sinner] should be encouraged to have certain positive outlets at hand which might serve as distractions. . . . television, a walk around the block, a telephone call or visit with friends, interesting reading matter or an absorbing hobby can all be used to drain off excessive libidinal impulses of the moment. . . . Certain traditional practices of battling the temptation are to be discouraged. To suggest, for example, that the adolescent wrap a rosary around his hand at bedtime, or make sure that his bed clothes and pajamas are not too tight, merely sets the stage for a frantic and fearful battle which the teenager will more often than not lose."
—Counselling the Catholic, 1959

"Among willing, nice young people, there are many who have fallen into habitual self-satisfaction, even though they recognize and accept its sinfulness. They suffer considerably from their failure. One must, above all, encourage them and protect them against capitulation. One must point out the 'no man's land' of sexuality. . . . Discipline of the imagination is of very special importance. . . . Every boy should resolve: I will not misuse my capacity for love."
—Modern Catholic Sex Instruction, 1964

Pope Sergius IV's nickname was *Bucca Porci*—"Pig's Snout."

"If a boy reads in the bathroom, and often masturbates there, he might stop reading at such times. If he doesn't read, and masturbates, perhaps he should take a book or magazine in with him."

—*Counselling the Catholic*

CASE STUDIES

"One day I was told by a girl student who had long been given to self-abuse: 'Since I threw myself, with all my energy, into scientific work and found satisfaction in that, I have ceased to practice self-abuse. I am aware, however, that the outwardly visible work I produce is nothing more than a different form of self-abuse—in fact mental and spiritual onanism.' Perhaps the girl was right because when she had exhausted her interest in science she began her self-abuse again."

—*The Problem of Onanism,* **by Frederick Von Gagern, 1954**

"In college I had a classmate who used to get so tense at exam time that study became impossible. The only way he could quiet his nerves for study was by masturbating. He is a priest, now, and I don't know anything about his personal habits but I do know that he seems to be doing great work with no signs of tension."

—*Binding with Briars,* **by Father Richard Ginder, 1975**

UPDATE

"[The Vatican] recently reasserted that masturbation was indeed a grave sin, but few Catholic moralists today outside of Rome would be prepared to agree. . . . There is relatively little evidence that the early Christian writers were concerned about this kind of behavior, and indeed it was with considerable difficulty that Saint Alphonsus Liguori [the father of anti-masturbationism] managed to persuade the teachers of his era that it was a problem that should be taken seriously. . . . "

—*Everything You Wanted to Know About the Catholic Church but Were Too Pious to Ask,* **by Andrew Greeley, 1978**

Q: How many popes have given themselves double names?

IF YOU MARRY
OUTSIDE THE FAITH

What happens if you marry a non-Catholic? Today it's no big deal, but in the pre-Vatican II days, it could get you kicked out of the church. Here's what the Baltimore Catechism *had to say about "mixed marriages."*

Q. 1036. Does the Church forbid the marriage of Catholics with persons who have a different religion or no religion at all?
A. Yes. . . . Such marriages generally lead to indifference, loss of faith, and to the neglect of the religious education of the children.

Q. 1039. What are the conditions upon which the Church will permit a Catholic to marry one who is not a Catholic?
A. (1) That the Catholic be allowed the free exercise of his or her religion; (2) that the Catholic shall try by teaching and good example to lead the one who is not a Catholic to embrace the true faith; (3) that all the children born of the marriage shall be brought up in the Catholic religion. . . . Without these promises, the Church will not consent to a mixed marriage, and if the Church does not consent the marriage is unlawful.

Q. 1043. Does the Church seek to make converts by its laws concerning mixed marriages?
A. The Church . . . seeks only to keep its children from losing their faith and becoming perverts by constant company with persons not Catholic. The Church does not wish persons to become Catholics merely for the sake of marrying Catholics. Such conversions are, as a rule, not sincere, do no good, but rather make such converts hypocrites and guilty of greater sins, especially sacrilege.

Q. 1040. What penalty does the Church impose on Catholics who marry before a Protestant minister?

A: Only 2—John Paul I (1978) and John Paul II.

A. Catholics who marry before a Protestant minister incur excommunication . . . because by such a marriage they make profession of a false religion in acknowledging as a priest one who has neither sacred power nor authority.

Q. 1041. How does the Church show its displeasure at mixed marriages?
A. The Church shows its displeasure at mixed marriages by the coldness with which it sanctions them, prohibiting all religious ceremony by forbidding the priest to use any sacred vestments, holy water or blessing of the ring at such marriages; by prohibiting them also from taking place in the Church or even in the sacristy. On the other hand, the Church shows its joy and approval at a true Catholic marriage by the Nuptial Mass and solemn ceremonies.

. . . CATHOLIC COLOR CODES
What do different colors symbolize in Christian art and culture? Some colors have obvious meanings; others are pretty surprising:

Black: Death, Satan, the underworld, witchcraft, and mourning.

White: Innocence, purity, holiness, and light.

Black *and* white together: Humility or purity (some religious orders, such as the Augustinians, the Dominicans, and some Benedictines, wear black-and-white habits).

Sky Blue: Truth, heaven, love, the Virgin Mary.

Brown: Spiritual death and degradation (brown habits symbolize renunciation of worldly pleasures).

Yellow: Sometimes it symbolizes the sun, divinity, sacredness, or revealed truth; other times it means jealousy, treason, and dishonesty (Judas is often depicted wearing yellow clothing).

President John F. Kennedy made his Catholic secret service agents go to confession

MORE CHAPTER
AND VERSE

Here's another batch of unusual New Testament passages:

MORE MIXED MESSAGES

Jesus in the Sermon on the Mount: "You have heard that it was said to the men of old, 'You shall not kill; and whoever kills shall be liable to judgment.' But I say to you that every one who is angry with his brother shall be liable to judgment; whoever insults his brother shall be liable to the council, and whoever says 'You fool!' shall be liable to the hell of fire."

—Matthew 5:21-22

"While [Jesus] was speaking, a Pharisee asked him to dine with him; so he went in and sat at table. The Pharisee was astonished to see that he did not first wash before dinner. And the Lord said to him, 'Now you Pharisees cleanse the outside of the cup and of the dish, but inside you are full of extortion and wickedness. You fools!' "

—Luke 11:37-40

STRANGE ADVICE

"[Jesus] also said to the disciples, 'There was a rich man who had a steward, and charges were brought to him that this man was wasting his goods. And he called him and said to him, 'What is this that I hear about you? Turn in the account of your stewardship, for you can no longer be steward.' And the steward said to himself, 'What shall I do, since my master is taking the stewardship away from me? I am not strong enough to dig, and I am ashamed to beg. I have decided what to do, so that people may receive me into their houses when I am put out of the stewardship.' So summoning

at the same time he did. Why? He didn't want his priest to recognize his voice.

his master's debtors one by one, he said to the first, 'How much do you owe my master?' He said 'A hundred measures of oil.' And he said to him, 'Take your bill, and sit down quickly and write fifty.' Then he said to another, 'And how much do you owe?' He said, 'A hundred measures of wheat.' He said to him, 'Take your bill, and write eighty.' The master commended the dishonest steward for his shrewdness; for the sons of this world are more shrewd in dealing with their own generation than the sons of light. And I tell you, make friends for yourselves by means of unrighteous [money], so that when it fails they may receive you into eternal habitations."

—Luke 16:1-9

NO TIME TO WASTE

"As they were going along the road, a man said to [Jesus], 'I will follow you wherever you go.' And Jesus said to him, 'Foxes have holes, and birds of the air have nests; but the Son of man has nowhere to lay his head.' To another he said, 'Follow me.' But [the man] said, 'Lord, let me first go and bury my father.' But [Jesus] said to him, 'Leave the dead to bury their own dead; but as for you, go and proclaim the kingdom of God.' Another said, 'I will follow you, Lord: but let me first say farewell to those at my home.' Jesus said to him, 'No one who puts his hand to the plow and looks back is fit for the kingdom of God.' "

—Luke 9:57-62

✠ ✠ ✠

. . . ONE LAST THOUGHT

"And [Jesus] said, 'Woe to you lawyers also! For you load men with burdens hard to bear, and you yourselves do not touch the burdens with one of your fingers.' "

—Luke 11:46-52

Why is Pope Leo I (440-461) known as Leo "the Great?" Among other things,

CATHOLIC QUIZ #4
THE SINGING NUN

*She's mostly forgotten now, but in the 1960s the Singing Nun
was probably the most famous Catholic in the world after JFK
and the pope. Let's take a minute to sing her praises.*

T OP NUN
Remember the *Ed Sullivan Show*? If you had tuned in to
watch it one particular evening in 1963, you would have
seen a peculiar sight: a Belgian nun in full habit playing a guitar
and singing a song called "Dominique." The nun's name was
Sister Luc-Gabrielle, but she was better known as *Soeur Sourire*
("Sister Smile")—and her song was fast becoming a pop music hit
all over the world.

Hardly anyone who tuned in that night had any idea what
Soeur Sourire was singing—"Dominique's" lyrics were entirely in
French. But that didn't matter: The tune's light melody was so
catchy that the song went all the way to number one on U.S. pop
music charts, displacing artists as famous as Stevie Wonder and
the Beatles and ultimately selling more than 1.5 million copies.
The song was a critical success as well, winning the 1963
Grammy for the best religious song and numerous other awards.
Soeur Sourire became a star in her own right—her fame peaked
in 1966, when Debbie Reynolds portrayed her in the film *The
Singing Nun*.

QUESTION TIME
*Now that your memory has been jogged a little, see how well you can
answer the following questions (answers are on page 201):*

1. How was Soeur Sourire discovered?

he met with Attila the Hun personally and talked him out of pillaging Rome.

(A) A Philips record company executive heard her singing at Mass . . . and signed her to a record contract on the spot.

(B) Nuns from her religious order talked the Philips record company into making an album of her songs so that they would have something to give to children during religious retreats.

(C) Eager to cash in on the excitement generated by Vatican II, the Philips record company held a music contest for nuns . . . and Sister Luc-Gabrielle won. First prize: a $100,000 donation to the winner's favorite religious charity, and a record contract.

2. What was the song "Dominique" about?

(A) It was about the time her convent dumped Thursday night bingo in favor of Tuesday night dominos, a *unique* innovation that she nicknamed *dominique* (domino plus unique).

(B) It was a tribute to the early gospel career of rock 'n' roll legend Fats Domino, who got his start singing in church. Soeur Sourire met him during a civil rights march in the late 1950s and was so impressed with his musical talent and passion for social justice that she wrote her first song in his honor.

(C) It was a tribute to the inventor of rosary beads.

3. How well was the album initially received in the United States?

(A) It flopped.

(B) It was an overnight hit.

(C) It was an overnight hit—but only because Pope Paul VI praised it publicly during a papal audience with *American Bandstand* host Dick Clark.

4. What was her next big attempt at a song hit?

(A) "Monique" (it bombed).

(B) "Plastique" (it *literally* bombed).

(C) "Unique" (it was one of a kind . . . but it still bombed).

(D) "Glory Be to God for the Golden Pill" (the public wouldn't swallow it).

5. What did she do with the money she made from the song?

(A) She donated it to her convent.

(B) She founded the Domino's Pizza chain.

(C) She blew it all playing bingo in Las Vegas with Elvis Presley and Col. Tom Parker. (The King helped her make the money back by recording a version of "Dominique" on the B side of his hit single "Hunk-a Burnin' Love.")

✠ ✠ ✠

. . . SOME INSIDE DOPE ON POPES

Is the pope just a pope? Nope—here are the Holy Father's other titles:

Bishop of Rome
Vicar of Jesus Christ
Successor of Saint Peter, Prince of the Apostles
Supreme Pontiff
Patriarch of the West
Primate of Italy
Servant of the Servants of God
Archbishop and Metropolitan of the Roman Province
Sovereign of the State of Vatican City

first person to describe the church as "catholic."

BORROWED TIMES

You know that Christmas Day falls on December 25 and that Easter falls in March or April . . . but do you know why? If not, you're in for a surprise.

PAPAL PROBLEM SOLVING
Suppose for a moment that you have just been elected the new pope of the Roman Catholic Church—and that you have made it the goal of your papacy to convert the entire United States to Catholicism by the year 2015. But there are a couple of snags in your plan: (1) You're competing against other religions who have the same goal in mind; (2) a recent poll has shown that few if any Americans would join a religion that doesn't celebrate the Fourth of July; and (3) the Catholic Church doesn't celebrate the Fourth of July.

. . . Still, you're not completely out of luck: July 4 *is* the feast day of Saint Ulric of Augsburg, an obscure saint that hardly anybody remembers anymore. What would you do—would you abandon America to some false pagan faith . . . or would you elevate Saint Ulric's Day to the status of a full-blown Catholic holiday?

The Dating Game
This scenario may seem ridiculous, but it's a lot like the situation the Catholic Church faced in the centuries following the Roman Empire's legalization of Christianity in 313 A.D. The church wanted to increase its membership (or at the very least, keep other religions from raiding its flock), but it quickly discovered that it isn't easy making Catholics out of people who are perfectly happy in some other religion. One of the biggest obstacles was that pagans and other unbelievers liked celebrating certain days as holidays and weren't about to change. So rather than fight them, the church decided to join them: It literally *created* holidays on cer-

tain dates for the sole purpose of making Christianity more popular to prospective converts. Some examples:

CHRISTMAS

Pagan Origin: December 25 was originally *Natalis Solis Invicti*, the Birthday of the Invincible Sun, the god Mithra.

Background: Mithraism, a Persian religion that spread to the Roman Empire in the first century A.D, was an extremely popular faith and early Christianity's biggest rival. Rather than try to stamp it out entirely, some time around the year 354 the church declared that Mithra's birthday also happened to be the birthday of Christ, even though no one knew for sure. Christians began commemorating the event with a special Christ Mass, piously asserting that "we hold this day holy, not like the pagans because of the birth of the sun, but because of him who made it."

Birthday Note: Fudging the Lord's birthday for the purpose of gaining converts may seem like a terrible sin today, but in the fourth century A.D. it was no big deal. In those days it was a person's *death* day that mattered; except for kings, in most cases birthdays weren't even recorded. Jesus probably didn't know his own birthdate (which most contemporary estimates place at the end of May) . . . and almost certainly never celebrated it. Thus to the early church fathers, misstating a completely insignificant date in order to spread the faith seemed like a pretty good trade-off.

EASTER

Pagan Origin: Easter takes its name from *Eastre*, the pagan goddess of spring. During Eastre, Roman pagans venerated the *hare* (Eastre's earthly symbol and the direct ancestor of today's Easter bunny) and exchanged dyed eggs, which symbolized new life.

Background: Beginning in the second century A.D., Christian missionaries took advantage of the fact that the resurrection of

A. Confraternity of Christian Doctrine.

Jesus fell on about the same date that pagans celebrated the festival of Eastre . . . and started holding their own celebrations on the same date in the hopes of winning converts.

Holiday Note: Easter remained a relatively obscure holiday in the United States until the Civil War, when the notion of resurrection that the holiday represented became a means by which Americans could cope with the massive casualties caused by the war.

SAINT VALENTINE'S DAY

Pagan Origin: The festival of *Lupercus*, which marked the passage of adolescent boys into adulthood, was celebrated in the Roman Empire as far back as the fourth century B.C. The festival honored the Roman god Lupercus, who protected the faithful from wolves.

Background: One of the most popular (and most lust-filled) Lupercus traditions was a lottery in which young men drew the names of adolescent females from a box. Whatever girl the young man picked would be his "partner" for a year, a relationship that was often sexual. (What happened at the end of the year? The kids held another lottery…and the process started all over again.)

The early church hated the holiday for obvious reasons, and in 496 A.D. Pope Gelasius outlawed it. In its place he substituted Saint Valentine's Day, named in honor of an obscure bishop martyred in 270 A.D. for marrying young lovers at a time when the Roman Empire forbade marriage. Gelasius dumped the old lottery in favor of a new one in which both men and women drew the names of saints . . . and spent the rest of the year trying to emulate their lives. The new holiday wasn't nearly as much fun as the one it replaced, yet somehow it persisted.

NEW YEAR'S DAY

Pagan Origin: In 153 B.C. the Roman Senate changed New

More than 20 European churches claim to possess

Year's Day from March 25, the first day of spring, to January 1. The Roman Empire converted to Christianity in 313 A.D.; even so, it continued to celebrate New Year's Day in defiance of the Catholic Church's efforts to abolish all pagan holidays and rituals.

Background: The Catholic Church (which did not celebrate *any* day as New Year's Day) combatted the January 1 celebrations by proclaiming the feast of Christ's Circumcision on that date and organizing new celebrations around the new theme. (Declaring January 1 as Jesus' circumcision date made perfect sense from a religious standpoint: Jewish infants are traditionally circumcised seven days after birth . . . and January 1 falls seven days after December 25.)

The date is still recognized as a holiday by Catholics, Lutherans, Episcopalians, and other branches of Christianity, although in 1970 the Catholic Church cut out the reference to Christ's foreskin and replaced it with a slightly less graphic feast known as the solemnity of Mary, Mother of God.

Holiday Note: For years the early church forbade its members from using images of the New Year's Babe—the infant counterpart to Father Time—in its celebrations. It finally relented and permitted the effigy . . . on the condition that worshippers used a representation of the infant Jesus.

APRIL FOOL'S DAY

Pagan Origin: April 1 falls exactly seven days after March 25, which the Romans considered New Year's Day up until the year 153 B.C.

Background: The *Romans* may have made the switch in 153 B.C. . . . but the *French* held on to March 25 until 1564 A.D., when King Charles IX adopted the Gregorian calendar (named for Pope Gregory XIII) and ordered that New Year's Day be moved to January 1. But his decision hardly suited bon vivants, drunkards, and others used to throwing parties during the week

relics containing milk from the Virgin Mary's breasts.

ending April 1; they continued their celebrations as if nothing had changed. More serious Frenchmen mocked them by exchanging foolish gifts and pulling practical jokes on April 1. In time all of the celebrants became known as "April Fools," since their New Year's celebrations no longer fell on New Year's Day.

HALLOWEEN

Pagan Origin: Halloween is the direct descendant of an ancient Celtic holiday celebrated in Ireland on October 31 as far back at the fifth century B.C.

Background: The Celts of Ireland believed that on October 31 anyone who had died in the previous year selected the body of an animal or person to inhabit for the next coming twelve months, after which the spirit passed into the afterlife. The Celts protected themselves from such possession by dressing in scary costumes . . . and by burning to death any person or animal who appeared to be possessed.

Note: Technically speaking, Halloween is not a Catholic holiday: The Church never officially adopted the Celtic version or created its own holiday to compete against it. The *name* "Halloween" is Catholic, though: October 31 falls on the evening ("e'en") before All Saints Day, which used to be known as All Hallows' Day.

✣   ✣   ✣

...BOOK NOTES

"There are six sorts of bad books:
1. Books which are plainly about very bad things; 2. many novels; 3. idle books; 4. bad newspapers and journals; 5. superstitious books; 6. Protestant books and tracts."

> —*Tracts for Spiritual Reading,* by Reverend J. Furniss, a ninteenth-century priest and children's author.

THE ANSWER PAGES

Here are the solutions to the quiz pages.
How well did you do?

AT THE OSCARS QUIZ, PAGE 44

1. (B) Julie Andrews, who played Maria von Trapp, described it as "awfully saccharine"—and Christopher Plummer, who played Georg von Trapp, gave it the nickname *The Sound of Mucus*. (He nearly quit when he found out studio officials were going to dub out his singing voice; but studio executives convinced him to stay.) According to one report, the movie bombed in Salzburg, Austria, where most of the location work was filmed. But it was a hit with the American public—*The Sound of Music* was the most successful film of 1965 and cemented Andrews's status as a superstar . . . although coming just one year after her Oscar-winning performance in *Mary Poppins*, it resulted in her being typecast in goodie-goodie roles for nearly twenty years. (Change of pace: Her next big role was in the 1982 film *Victor/Victoria*, in which she played a woman who impersonates a gay male singer to make ends meet. Andrews was nominated for Best Actress but lost to Meryl Streep in *Sophie's Choice*).

2. (C) Bing Crosby played Father Charles Francis Patrick O'Malley (whom one critic described as "the kindest, singingest priest to ever grace the screen") in *Going My Way* (1944) and *The Bells of St. Mary's* (1945). Crosby was perfect for the part. "Bing just played Bing Crosby," his brother Bob told an interviewer in 1989, "because he went to Jesuit school all his life." *Going My Way* was Crosby's first dramatic role—it established him as a superstar actor and crooner and won him the 1944 Academy Award for Best Actor. (He lost the 1945 Best Actor to Ray Milland's performance in *The Lost Weekend*.)

3. (A) Fitzgerald played Father Fitzgibbon alongside Bing Crosby's

Father O'Malley . . . and lost the Best Actor award to the crooner. He did win Best Supporting Actor, though; *Going My Way*, which was nominated for ten Oscars, won seven. Fitzgerald's nomination for two Oscars for the same part was unprecedented—not to mention a source of some embarrassment for the Motion Picture Academy: That year it changed the rules so that the anomaly would never happen again.

4. (B) Nominated for twelve Oscars, the film won four. Even so, reviews were mixed: The *New York Times* described it as "tedious and repetitious . . . and it goes in for dialectic discourse that will clutter and fatigue the average mind."

5. (C) Twentieth Century-Fox had such little faith in the *Miracle on 34th Street* that it released it in *July* instead of December; nevertheless, it went on to become one of the most popular Christmas films in history.

6. (A) When Twentieth Century Fox released *The Song of Bernadette*, it set out to give the film snob appeal by showing it only in selected theatres (probably in towns with large Catholic populations) and by charging a higher ticket price than they did with most films. The prestige strategy helped make the film a big hit . . . but it backfired on award night. According to *Inside Oscar: The Unofficial History of the Academy Awards*, "At Oscar time, *Bernadette* was still in limited release at advanced ticket prices, which meant that those [in the Academy] with the bulk of the voting power—the extras—had not yet been able to afford to go to the movie. A poll of voting extras showed that only 25% had seen *Bernadette*, whereas nearly all of them had seen—and voted for—*Casablanca*."

7. (C) The Academy agreed to fix the mistake free of charge—but a few days later MGM announced that the new inscription was being made out to the real Father Flanigan . . . and that Tracy had "donated" the statue to the real Boys' Town in Nebraska. The actor was furious. "Hold on a minute," he shouted to the MGM publicist who had given his statue away, "I won it. I want to keep it." "But you have another one," the publicist insisted. (Tracy had won Best Actor in 1937 for *Captains Courageous*—the only actor in history to win Best Actor two years in a row.) But Tracy was adamant. "Not unless the Academy gives me another one to keep myself." (It did . . . and Boys' Town got its Oscar).

8. (B) In its day, the parting of the Red Sea was the most sophisticated special effect ever attempted. "To get the effect," Susan Sackett writes in her book *Box Office Hits*, "shots of the actual Red Sea were matched with shots of dump tanks pouring huge amounts of water into a Paramount tank set. When the footage was reversed, the waters seemed to part. The careful blending of these two shots produced the desired effect. The combined footage took 18 months to film, at a cost of $1 million." (Nominated for seven Academy Awards, *The Ten Commandments* won only one.)

9. (B) Filmed at a cost of more than $15 million, *Ben Hur* was the most expensive movie in history up to that time, requiring five years of planning, fifty-thousand extras, one hundred thousand costumes, and three hundred sets, the largest of which was a sprawling eighteen acres. The chariot scene alone cost $1 million and took more than eight *months* to finish. But the sacrifice was worth it—the film was nominated for twelve Oscars and won eleven, more than any other film in Hollywood history.

10. (B) Thanks to wartime rationing of strategic materials, all of the Oscar statues awarded during World War II were made of plaster, with the understanding that the winners could exchange them for the genuine article once the war was over. Fitzgerald decapitated his a few hours after the ceremony while practicing his golf swing in his living room. (No need to feel sorry for him, though: Paramount Pictures bought him a new one the next day. Replacement cost: ten dollars.)

(also the name of a pagan god), was considered too inappropriate for a pope.

THE FLYING NUN QUIZ, PAGE 86

1. (D) TV executive Max Wylie was flipping through a Doubleday catalog of recently published books one day in the mid-1960s looking for ideas for TV sitcoms. He came across a book called *The Fifteenth Pelican,* a story about a ninety-pound nun who could fly. Author Tere Rios got the idea for the book while travelling through in 1955. "I saw a little Sister of Charity in her big white bonnet nearly blown off her feet in Paris," she later told reporters.

Wylie pitched the idea to Harry Ackerman, creator of the *Bewitched* TV series. Another show of his, *Gidget,* had just gone off the air and he was looking for a new vehicle for Sally Field, the star of the show. *Bewitched,* about a friendly witch with magic powers, had been a huge success; so had *I Dream of Jeanie,* a show about a female genie with magical powers who marries an astronaut. Ackerman thought a similar show about a nun would be a hit . . . although he worried that giving a nun magical powers would be too controversial. So he stuck with *The Fifteenth Pelican's* original premise and gave the nun special powers (brought on by high winds, her coronet, and the laws of aerodynamics) instead of magic ones.

2. (C) "I didn't want to play a nun," Field told *TV Guide* in 1968. "You're not allowed to kiss or show your belly button." But that wasn't her only objection: *Gidget* had fallen flat on its face, and Field mistakenly thought it was her fault. As *TV Guide* put it, "Sally came away with the feeling that she was somehow responsible for *Gidget's* flop and no one would tell her why. . . . She left the studio 'feeling defeated' . . . and embarked on a movie career, determined that TV should never darken her door again."

3. (B) Field tried out for the part of daughter Elaine Robinson in *The Graduate* . . . but Katherine Ross got the part. Then she tried out for the role of Neely in *Valley of the Dolls* . . . and lost it to Patty Duke. All of a sudden, another TV series didn't look so

Seeing it as a sign of "the anger of God," in 1456 Pope Calistus III (1455-1458)

bad. "It was presumptuous to think I could step into movies," Field later recalled. " 'Idiot,' I told myself, 'you're not Liz Taylor!' The Flying Nun would give me time to learn and still keep me in the public eye. So—I changed my mind." (Studio executives cemented the deal by raising her pay from her $450-a-week *Gidget* salary to $4,000 a week.)

4. (B)

5. (C) Studio executives were extremely worried about potential Catholic objections to *The Flying Nun* and went to great lengths to see that the church was not offended. They even gave special sneak previews of the pilot episode to high church officials all over the country, hoping to enlist their support for the show. "We just wanted to be sure the Catholic community dug it," one of the show's promoters told TV Guide in 1968.
　. . . But their concerns were ungrounded: Catholic Church officials *loved* the show and actually saw it as a much-needed recruiting film for nuns, whose numbers had been in decline since Vatican II. "The show is positioning nuns as human beings," one official with the National Catholic Office for Radio and Television said. "Only the studio, the agencies and the sponsors were worried. I guess they thought Catholics might stop buying toothpaste."

AT THE MOVIES QUIZ, PAGE 131
1. (C) No word on why they thought the church would find *Going My Way* offensive, but their fears were completely ungrounded—Pope Pius XII himself saw the film and liked it so much that he bought a copy for his own personal use.

2. (A) Jones' marriage was on the rocks . . . and rumors had sur-faced linking her romantically to movie producer David O. Selznick, whom she would later marry. Twentieth Century-Fox was so concerned about her marital status that they ordered her

issued a papal bull instructing Christians to pray for protection from Halley's comet.

to conceal the fact that she had a husband and two children. The ruse worked: most of the public thought she was single.

. . . But there was an even more controversial casting choice in the film, that of Linda Darnell as the Virgin Mary. Darnell was no virgin—she was the mistress of Twentieth Century-Fox president Daryl Zanuck, hardly the kind of woman to play the Mother of Jesus. The studio avoided scandal by leaving Darnell's name off the credits, a scheme that apparently worked: As the *Hollywood Reporter* observed in 1943, "The Catholic churches throughout the nation over the weekend appealed to their congregations to go see *The Song of Bernadette*," which helped make the film the fourth most successful film of 1943.

3. (B) Pope Leo XIII (1878-1903) was so impressed with *Ben-Hur*, a novel about a Jewish nobleman who is betrayed by the Roman governor and ultimately wins revenge, that he conferred a special blessing upon it in 1880.

4. (C) The movie was probably the most embarrassing of her career—even many Elvis fans admitted *Change of Habit* was a dud. As film critic Michael Medved put it, "With her whining voice, cutie-pie makeup and flirtatious manners, Sister Mary . . . is badly miscast as a sister of mercy, but not nearly so badly as her costar, Elvis Presley, who is expected to play a dedicated young M.D. who has pledged to bring medical care and rock 'n roll to the poor, deprived youth of the ghetto."

5. (B) So many newspapers and television stations (not to mention ABC, CBS, and NBC) refused to air commercials for *The Pope Must Die* that Miramax films hired Harvard law professor Alan Dershowitz to file a First Amendment lawsuit against the media, alleging infringement of its freedom of speech. But the company backed down a few weeks later and announced it had changed the name of the film to *The Pope Must Diet*. Fortunately for them, the film's star, Robbie Coltrane, was both overweight

The publicity pope: Pope John XXIII proclaimed St. Bernardine of

and clever—he was the one who suggested the change in the first place. "I can't take the credit really, except for my weight," the star later told reporters. "In London, someone went around with chalk and added the 'T' to the end of the title over my picture."

6. (A) Sinatra's performance was at least as bad as Mary Tyler Moore's in *Change of Habit*. *The New York Times* observed that "Frank Sinatra appears frightened speechless (and almost songless) by the task of playing a priest . . . the picture is so weighted with mawkish melancholia that it drips all over the screen." As *Cue* magazine put it, "The picture can be reasonably described as nauseating."

7. (B) Based on a play by Tennessee Williams that dealt with homosexuality and rape, *Streetcar* was attacked by film industry and Catholic Church censors, who insisted that more than nine minutes of the most offensive material be removed. Even censored, the film was pretty good: It won Best Actress, Best Supporting Actress, and Best Supporting Actor. (Marlon Brando lost the Best Actor Oscar to Humphrey Bogart's performance in *The African Queen*.)

8. (C) Tilly was nominated for her performance in *Agnes of God* (1985), in which she plays a childlike nun suspecting of murdering her newborn child. (She lost to Angelica Huston in *Prizzi's Honor*.)

THE SINGING NUN QUIZ, PAGE 187.

1. (B) As one nun told *Time* magazine in 1963, "We have these retreats for young girls at our Fichermont monastery, and in the evenings we sing songs composed by Sister Luc-Gabrielle. The songs are such a hit with our girls that they asked us to transcribe them." The nuns approached the Philips record company, and after a few months of prodding it agreed to let them use its

Siena the patron saint of public relations on May 20, 1960.

studios to record an album. Philips initially planned to issue only a few dozen pressings to the nuns for their own use, but company executives liked the album so much they contracted with the convent to sell it all over Europe.

2. (C) The song honors Saint Dominic Guzman, founder of the Dominican order and the man credited with introducing rosary beads (believed to be a Christian adaptation of Eastern prayer beads) to the Roman Catholic faith.

3. (A) When Philips issued Sister Luc-Gabrielle's album in Europe under the name *Soeur Sourire*, it took the continent by storm. But when it released it in the United States a few months later under the name *The Singing Nun*, no one bought it. . . . So Philips issued "Dominique" as a 45-r.p.m. single and sold more than four hundred thousand copies in three weeks.

4. (D) Soeur Sourire seemed to adjust quite well to her celebrity status at first . . . but it didn't last long: She left her convent in 1966 before taking her final vows, telling the press that she wanted to continue her missionary work while pursuing a recording career. No word on how well she succeeded as a missionary, but her singing career went bust. Her next big single, a tribute to artificial birth control titled "Glory Be to God for the Golden Pill," didn't have quite the same ring to it that "Dominique" had. Nobody bought it, nor did they buy the updated synthesizer version of "Dominique" that she issued in 1983.

5. (A) Sister Luc-Gabrielle did leave her convent in 1966, but not before she turned over all of her royalties to her religious order. The decision haunted her for the rest of her life: The Belgian government hounded her for $63,000 in back taxes for the next twenty years; and in 1983 a center for autistic children she and a friend (also an ex-nun) founded closed its doors due to lack of funds. Her life ended tragically in 1985 when she and the

Famous forgotten date: November 23, 1964, the last mandatory Latin

friend were found dead in their apartment, the victims of an apparent double suicide brought on by their financial problems. Soeur Sourire was fifty-one.

✠ ✠ ✠

HOLY GHOSTS

In 1258 King Louis IX of France gave six monks a house in the village of Chantilly to use as a monastery . . . but not long after they moved in, the monks decided they'd rather live in Vauvert, an abandoned palace located nearby. The only problem: They were afraid to ask the king for it directly. In his 1852 book *Extraordinary Popular Delusions and the Madness of Crowds*, Charles Mackay describes how the monks "set their ingenuity to work" and eventually got their hands on it:

> Almost immediately . . . frightful shrieks were heard to proceed from Vauvert at night; blue, red, and green lights were seen to glimmer from the windows . . . the clanking of chains was heard, and the howling as of persons in great pain. These disturbances continued for several months, to the great terror of all the country round, and even of the pious King Louis, to whom, at Paris, all the rumors were regularly carried with whole heaps of additions that accumulated on the way. At last a great spectre, clothed all in green, with a long white beard and a serpent's tail, took his station regularly at midnight in the principal window of the palace, howled fearfully, and shook his fists at passersby.
>
> The six monks at Chantilly . . . were exceedingly wrath that the devil should play such antics right opposite their dwelling, and hinted to the commissioners sent down by Saint Louis to investigate the matter, that if they were allowed to inhabit the palace, they would very soon make a clearance of the evil spirits. The king was quite charmed with their piety, and expressed to them how grateful he felt. . . . A deed was forthwith drawn up, and the palace of Vauvert became the property of the monks of St. Bruno. The disturbances ceased immediately, the lights disappeared, and the green ghost was laid at rest for ever.

Mass. From that day on, most masses were celebrated in the vernacular.

RECOMMENDED READING

A number of the chapters list books you can consult for further information. Here are some more great reading materials:

GENERAL REFERENCE

The Holy Bible, Revised Standard Version (Holman Bible Publishers, 1982)

The Catholic Encyclopedia, edited by Robert C. Broderick (Thomas Nelson Publishers, 1987)

A Concise History of the Catholic Church, by Thomas Bokenkotter (Doubleday, 1990)

Dynamic Catholicism, A Historical Catechism, by Thomas Bokenkotter (Doubleday, 1992)

Everything You Always Wanted to Know About the Catholic Church but Were Afraid to Ask for Fear of Excommunication, by Paul L. Williams (Doubleday, 1989)

Our Sunday Visitor's Catholic Encyclopedia, edited by Peter Stravinskas (Our Sunday Visitor, 1991)

1994 Catholic Almanac, by Felician A. Foy (Our Sunday Visitor, 1993), *updated every year*

POPES

The Oxford Dictionary of Popes, by J. N. D. Kelly (Oxford University Press, 1990)

Three Popes and the Jews, by Pinchas Lapide (Hawthorn Books, 1967)

Only about 3% of U.S. nuns are age 40 or younger.

SAINTS

A Guide to the Saints, by Kristen E. White (Ivy Books, 1991)

Making Saints: How the Catholic Church Determines Who Becomes a Saint, Who Doesn't, and Why, by Kenneth L. Woodward (Simon & Schuster, 1990)

A Dictionary of Saints, by Donald Attwater (Penguin, 1970)

The Pocket Dictionary of Saints, by John J. Delaney (Doubleday, 1983)

HUMOR

Growing Up Catholic, by Mary Jane Meara, Jeffrey Stone, Maureen Kelly, and Richard Davis (Doubleday, 1985). *See also* More Growing Up Catholic (1986) *and* Still Catholic After all These Years (1993), *by the same authors.*

Saints Preserve Us, by Sean Kelly and Rosemary Rogers (Random House, 1993)

MISCELLANEOUS

The Heretic's Handbook of Quotations: Cutting Comments on Burning Issues, edited by Charles Bufe (Tucson, AZ: Sharp Press, 1992)

In Search of Dracula (New York Graphic Society, 1972) and *Dracula: Prince of Many Faces* (Little, Brown, 1989), both by Radu Florescu and Raymond T. McNally

The Life and Death of Adolf Hitler, by Robert Payne (Military Heritage Press, 1989)

Adolf Hitler, by John Toland (Doubleday, 1976)

The Memoirs of Jacques Casanova de Seingalt, translated by Arthur Machen (1894). *Check your bookstore or public library for the latest reissue.*

The Massachusetts state legislature passed a "nunneries' inspection bill" in 1855.

ABOUT THE AUTHOR

John Dollison grew up in Lafayette, California. A former altar boy and CCD student, he graduated from De La Salle High School (run by the Christian Brothers) in 1985 and received a B.S. degree from the Haas School of Business at the University of California at Berkeley in 1989. This is his first book . . . but probably not his last.

Saint Joseph of Arimathaea is the patron saint of tin miners.